Tips, Tricks and Traps – Everything You Need To Know About Estate Agents

FIRST EDITION

P.Sheen

Dear PWC,

Thank you, for your time,

Pav Sheen

ISBN 978-0-9555537-1-4

Published By Ricsun Ltd. 2007

Printed in the United Kingdom.

Design by Ricsun Ltd.

First Edition 2007

Printed in the United Kingdom.

Available at www.BeatTheAgents.co.uk

CONTENTS

ACKNOWLEDGEMENTS   6
INTRODUCTION   7

<u>Buyers</u>

**1. What is an Estate Agent and What are his Key
     Characteristics?**   11

- What is an Estate Agent?   11
- Key Characteristics of an Estate Agent.   11
- Estate Agent Payment Structure   12
- Estate Agent Target Structure   13
- The Ability to Lie   13
- Power of Creativity   14
- Closing   15

**2. First Contact with an Estate Agent and Building
     the Rapport**   18

- First Impressions   19
- The Process   20
- Open and Quality Questions   21
- Succeeding Where Others have Failed   24
- The Agent's Approach to What you Want   26
- Pre-selling   27
- Under Promising and Over Delivering   30
- Closing an Applicant for Viewings   30
- Using Fear Of Loss and Urgency   33

3. The Viewing Process   37

- Block Viewings   37
- Ways to Book Viewings   38
- Viewing the Property   39
- Previous Offers   40
- Selling During the Viewing - The Demonstration   41

•	Emotion Spotting	43
•	Closing the Applicant into an Offer	45
•	Office Assistance	47
•	Accompanying Closes	49

4. Negotiating the Price - The Deal   **58**

•	The Time Game	58
•	The Silent Close	59
•	The Compliment Close	60
•	Gazumping	62
•	Tips on How to Avoid Gazumping	63

5. Estate Agency and Mortgages   **65**

•	Brokers - Why they are in Agent's Offices and What are the Benefits to the Advisor?	65
•	The Estate Agent's Agenda	66
•	The Assumption Close	68
•	The Or Close	69
•	The Dual Close	70
•	Bargaining Chips	71

Sellers

6. The Valuation Process and First Impression   **75**

•	The Valuation Process and First impression	75
•	Booking and Pre-valuation Questions. Getting Your Private Details!	76
•	Overcoming the Fee	78

7. The Valuation   **80**

•	The Agent's Act	80
•	The Sale	81
•	The Price- How does an Agent come to the Valuation Price of your Home?	83

- Over-valuing to Increase the Agent's Chances of Getting the Property 84
- The Fee/the Commission 85
- Other Closes an Agent Could Use 87

8. Price Reductions and Illusion of Vendor Care 95

- Mock Viewing and Negative Feedback 95
- Vendor Care Calls 97
- Fake Offers for a Price Reduction 99

9. Other Sales Tools an Estate Agent May Use 101

- Words – 7% 101
- Socio-linguistics /Voice Quality and Tone – 38% 103
- Physiology – 55% 104
- Humour 104

10. Estate Agents and Their Relationships 106

- Relationships with Investors 106
- To What Lengths will an Estate Agent go to get the Best Price? He Undervalues! 107
- Relationships with Recommended Conveyancers 108
- Relationships with Timber and Damp Specialists, Roof Specialists, Plumbers and Electricians 109

11. Introduction to Home Information Pack (H.I.P) 111

- What is the H.I.P? 111
- The Pros of the H.I.P 112
- The Cons of the H.I.P 112

ACKNOWLEDGEMENTS

Firstly I would like to thank God for all I have been given in life and the ability to write this book.

I would like to say thank you to those estate agents that drove me to write this book. Without you underhandedness, lack of respect and disregard for other peoples feelings I would never have been inspired.

I would like to say thank you to my mother, father, brothers Rick and Zeus for supporting and always believing in me. I would also like to say thank you to my good friend Roger Davids for all his input and insight into this book. Without you this would never have been possible!

I would like to thank Big Dad for his support, love and wisdom throughout my life and Papaji for all his support and concern for my well being.

I would like to thank Big Mum for all her strength, support and love growing up. I would like to thank Bibi for all her love and warm hugs.

Thank you Dave, Thomas, Daniel, Raks, Mary & Nick for always being supportive friends.

I would like to thank my mentor and teacher J.Wilkinson for all the help he has given me throughout my life.

I would like to thank my other teachers, mentors and people who have had great influence in my life, Mr.Tardios, Mrs.Tardios, the late Madame Langlois, Navdeep, Navneet & Navkirn.

Thank you to the Dhanoa, Sekhon, Dhaliwal, Bria, Breyal, Kooner, Bajwa, Sandhu and Athwal Families.

And last but not least I'd like to thank you for buying a copy of my book.

Thank you all.

INTRODUCTION

Have you ever wondered what your estate agent was thinking?
What tricks, traps and tactics he's using on you without your knowledge?
Have you ever lost out on a property because of an estate agent, or feared that had you paid over the odds?
Have you ever been Gazumped or wish you had known what to look out for so you could have seen it coming and put a stop to it?
Has your property been sitting on the market for weeks due to false promises so that you ended up having to sell it for less?
Have you ever sold your property for less than what it was worth because maybe an estate agent had undervalued it so he could offer it to his investors and earn back-handers?

In March 2006 there was a programme televised by the **BBC** called *The Secret Agent* where a reporter went undercover into the world of estate agency and exposed the unethical inner workings of some estate agents in the U.K. This documentary opened the eyes of the public and for many of us confirmed our thoughts about some of these so-called professionals. Nearly a year later in February 2007 another programme was televised by **ITV** called **Confessions of an Estate Agent** which heard the confessions of some estate agents and ways in which they abused the trust put in them by the their clients. However as much of an eye opener as these programmes were, many of us are still falling victim to the Tricks and Traps of these estate agents and there is little being done to regulate such a problem.

Tips Tricks and Traps – Everything You Need to Know About Estate Agents, is arguably the first book written for buyers and sellers about estate agents in England and

Wales. This book was not written to improve the image of estate agents. The purpose of this book is to expose the tactics estate agents use to dupe us. As well as this, it provides useful tips on how to avoid each trick and trap and turn the tables on these estate agents by revealing all their secrets. Its purpose is to give you, the buyers and sellers, the upper hand for a change and to furnish you with a tool which is always to hand in each situation. It will give you an insight into the world of estate agency such as you never had before.

This book will be able to answer all the questions above as well as any others you may have about estate agents and enable you to anticipate most of the problems you are likely to encounter in dealing with them. It covers the various stratagems an estate agent will go through including all the underhanded tactics he may use to direct you towards a specific objective whilst maintaining his agenda and lining his pockets.

The book itself is divided into two sections. The first section is for **buyers**. It covers topics such as how an estate agent gains your trust, the tactics he uses to get you out viewing, how an estate agent may close you into offering on a property; how he uses your emotions and other bargaining chips against you and how he gets you to increase your offer so that the final purchase price is higher than what you really could have bought it for.

The second section is for **sellers**. It talks about how an estate agent begins to dissect a prospective seller from first point of contact, tactics he may use on a valuation to close you into signing with his company, how estate agents overvalue your property just to get it onto the market and how then they will use vendor care to get you to reduce the price of an overvalued property once they have got a signed contract.

Within the sections each chapter represents a stage of the process estate agents will undergo with you. It will show how they use timing, structure and tactics to gain your trust, get you into a position where you feel comfortable enough to offer or sign, and ways in which they use words and phrases subconsciously to direct you towards serving their agenda. But for every action there is an equal and opposite reaction. Therefore the book has been structured in such a way that wherever a situation may arise where one of these Tricks or Traps may be used, there is a useful Tip that counteracts these tactics. Each tip will allow you to foresee these tactics and their tell-tale signs so that you know what to avoid. At the same time these tips serve to advise you on what to do in each situation and thereby giving you the upper hand over the estate agent almost every time.

When people think of the most hated professions in the U.K, we think traffic wardens, Tele-sales reps and estate agents. Unfortunately there is little we can do to avoid the first two. However there are a few things that we the public can do when it comes to our dealings with estate agents.

Almost all of us who have purchased a house, have fallen victim to the estate agents` tricks and traps, whether we are aware of it or not. In some forms, we have been sold into the idea of offering on properties, dealing with in house financial advisors, putting our properties on the market with an agent, and, worst of all, being "Gazumped". Indeed our experiences with estate agents have convinced most of us that we never want to see another estate agent as long as we live. However, the problem still remains that we, as the general public whether we like it or not have to go through an estate agent to buy a house.

Certainly an agent can never decide for you what home you choose to buy, but they do have some unorthodox ways of nudging you into making that decision. What this book aims to do is make you, as a prospective buyer or seller, aware of such tactics, what to look out for and when these tricks may be used. I will give you a first-hand insight into the workings of an estate agent, in many common scenarios you will encounter, as a buyer or seller, from the minute you make first contact with him.

Awareness can be curative! So I hope that with the tips and knowledge provided by this book, the tables will finally turn and for a change we, the innocent public, will have a greater understanding of the world of estate agency, what to be aware of and how to remedy it.

So, in the famous words of many estate agents, " *let's crack on*".

Chapter 1

What is an Estate Agent and What Are His Key Characteristics?

What is an Estate Agent?

The dictionary defines an estate agent as "a person whose business is the sale or lease of buildings or land on behalf of others". But we know an estate agent here in England as something slightly different. Many of us have had bad experiences with estate agents and see them as crooked salespersons whom we would not trust if our lives depended on it.

A number of estate agents don't in fact have any particular education or qualifications for the job they do, so how do they become so-called "professionals" in their field of expertise?

Well, many estate agents are the result of conditioning young minds in a high-pressure sales environment to believe that targets and sales are of the highest priority. Failure to do this could often lead to criticism from their bosses, loss of earnings and in some cases even loss of employment.

So what are the key characteristics of an estate agent?

All estate agents have certain specific traits in common. Many have a strong work ethic and ambition to succeed. This is often accompanied by their ability to knuckle down and persist in a chosen direction until they have achieved their goal.

Although this is common among many young professionals trying to make their mark in the world, the estate agent sometimes uses unethical tactics to achieve his goals. It's these tactics that often cause a great amount of unnecessary anxiety to buyers and sellers and thus have become some of the most hated professionals in the country.

Many estate agents seem to conjure their "facts" out of thin air in order to create a foundation of trust. Some have the ability to produce an air of bluff integrity, while maintaining their agendas and intentions. While others have the ability to use your emotions against you and close you into purchasing one of their products. (And there are a few other tactics which approximate more nearly to the conjuror's sleight-of-hand.)

However, the most important motive that drives the agent to employ these tactics is **fear**. Many employers often instill an element of fear within the estate agent. "Many of us will often do more to avoid pain than we will to gain pleasure". (Anthony Robbins)

Fear is used is to make the estate agents believe that they will lose much more if they don't achieve their targets. They will lose money, reputation or the job as well as suffering disciplinary action from employers. The result is that the estate agent will be conditioned in such a way that in order to avoid this pain, he will do what it takes and feel as though his actions were justified regardless of the effects they may have on others.

What follows are a number of other factors that influence and accompany an estate agent's fear and further strengthen the psychology behind his approach.

Estate Agent Payment Structure

Many estate agents earn on a payment structure that entitles them to high commissions but a low basic wage. This means they have the ability to earn whatever they put in and make their own wages. But it also means that if they don't make their sales and targets, they go home with a wage that hardly justifies the sixty hours week. So they often do what they must to achieve that target regardless of the effects it may have on innocent parties, (i.e. buyers and sellers), otherwise they earn next to nothing.

Estate Agent Target Structure

Many estate agent works off sales targets as you know. Employers exert constant pressure upon their agents to achieve these targets.

A very common target that estate agents work by is the viewing to sales ratio. For example in a certain area a buyer may need to look at 10 properties before buying one; this means that the estate agent's target is to show 10 properties to achieve one sale. If an agent is expected to sell 10 properties in a month, then he must arrange at least 25 property viewing appointments a week, or 100 a month. Failure to do this could lead to loss of earnings, criticism and eventually loss of employment.

They also have to work against the other agents in the office, who all have the same driving force and conditioning, especially as commissions are only awarded to the agent who sells the property, and if they fail to reach targets and make sales they may even lose their jobs.

The Ability to Lie

As we have said an agent must also have the ability to lie and twist the truth in order to make a sale; it is all part and parcel of achieving the viewing to sales ratio.

For example –

" This property has just come on the market, you'll be the first to see it, it's the perfect house for you, when will you be free to have a look, Wednesday or Thursday?"

This property may well have been on the market for a number of weeks. However the agent has used a lie to get a viewing for a property. He's done this by highlighting the point that the property has only recently come on the market and that the potential buyer is getting exclusivity. He tried to make the buyer believe that they will be the first to view it and it's the perfect home for them. By inviting to view he has led them to believe that they will not only be able to buy their dream home, but purchase it before someone else does and not lose out on a unique opportunity to find their dream home.

Power of Creativity

Another characteristic an estate agent may possess is the power of creativity, another major tool he may use when gaining your trust, selling you a home or selling your home. An agent may at times create certain ideas in your mind that help to nudge you into offering on a property.

For example - if you go on a viewing with an estate agent, you may want to know what the area is like to which a common reply from the agent is, " It's fantastic, I've just bought a house about 5 minutes walk from here". Of course the estate agent is a professional and if he has a property nearby then the area must be good. You may even want him to prove it. At which point he may produce the keys to a vacant property on his books, take you there and make you believe he owns it.

Closing

Throughout the estate agent process there will be many different tools an agent may use to gain trust and manipulate a buyer or seller. One of the key tools and probably most important any salesperson will use is" the close". Throughout the book you will see many references to the sales tool known as "**closing**".

You may have heard of "closing" in other places, such as the Hollywood motion picture "Glen Garry Glenn Ross", a very popular film about real estate agents in the U.S and the tactics they use. A very famous sales term was used in this film called, "ABC- Always Be Closing" which became very highly used among sales professionals in the 90`s and is still used today by many sales companies in their training. The idea of always to be closing is one embraced by many estate agents.

But what is closing and how do estate agents use it?

"Closing" is a skill that is learnt by many estate agents to highlight the benefits of a particular property or service, as well as its advantages to you. At the same time the agent can use your emotions and any other beneficial factors available at the time as bargaining chips to manipulate you into going for the deal without your ever being aware of it.

For example –

In the event that you see a house you like, the agent may use a combination of lies and closes to nudge you into offering.

" Well John, you're the first to see this house and I brought you here first because I know you are a serious buyer. However if you want this property you need to make an offer, I can hold off all other viewing until 10am tomorrow but after that I know my colleague in the office has got a very interested couple who saw the board outside the house and wanted this area. And hey lets put it this way, if you buy this house you can always come over for a barbecue at my place anytime; as you know I live just 5 minutes from here".

As you can see the estate agent has used a combination of tactics. He's used a lie to secure John about the area by telling him he himself has a house close by, and then used a combination of the power of creativity with a fear of loss and urgency to close the buyer. He has done this by putting the idea in John's head that his colleague has another interested party and that he may lose the property if he does not offer. If John wants the property, he would have no other choice than to offer there and then.

The different types of closes, tricks and traps an estate agent is most likely to use will be illustrated in the following chapters.

Tip - Always remember that the estate agent's objective is to nudge you in the right direction based on his agenda and your love for the property; never give away too much. An agent will almost always see a buyer or seller in one way but with two equally beneficial results. To the agent we are all cattle, he can either grow us for produce and make his money off our milk or carve us up and sell us to a fast food chain, either way he makes his money, and unfortunately for many of us its usually the latter.

N.B. the estate agent will see you as a client until he can categorise you. Once you are categorised he will assign you a title; an Applicant is a prospective buyer (once you have offered you will be regarded as a Buyer as opposed to an Applicant) and a Potential Vendor is a prospective seller. Throughout the book I have used this

terminology so remember that if you're looking to buy then I'm referring to you as an Applicant or Potential/ Prospective Buyer. If you're considering selling then you're a prospective Vendor until you come onto the market with an estate agent at which point you will become the Vendor.

Chapter 2

First Contact with an Estate Agent and Building the Rapport

For many of us calling into an estate agent's office is quite a common thing when we are looking for a property. It's a simple process by which we enter the office, give our details, tell the agent what we want and see if they have it on their books, and if they don't have what we want, then get them to give us a call when they do have it.

But for the agent, the process is viewed in a slightly different light. Not only is the agent taking down your details and learning about what you would like. But, it is a vital time for the agent to begin assessing you, gaining your trust and sowing certain seeds that may help him in the future when it comes to selling you the products he has to offer.

This chapter is about the way in which an estate agent will build a rapport with you, how an agent uses questions to his advantage and the ways in which an agent will attempt to get you out viewing properties. It will allow you to see the process an agent will go through with you and why.

Key Tip - Almost every single thing an agent says is pre-planned words or phrases used to maximise their chances to gain your trust and in turn to achieve his objectives. It is very important for an estate agent to become on a first name basis with you. This is one of the tools the agent may use to help him overcome our preconceived ideas and/or the bad reputation he may actually have. His aim is for you to see him as a friend and someone who can advise you and help you find what you are looking for, as opposed to a witty and

18

crafty sales professional with his own agenda. It may seem trivial but it does work.

This section will highlight how an agent will achieve some of his objectives, and the benefits he will gain through the process of registering you as an applicant.

First Impressions

Most people who call into or phone estate agents offices already have a preconceived view of agents and are aware of their bad reputation. An estate agent also knows this, and that it is the first barrier he must overcome if he is to sell his products. To an agent, the first impression he gives out is a key component.

The first impression process begins from the first point of contact, be it a phone call or a client that walks through the door. As in many places of business a greeting at the front door is a common occurrence, but with the estate agent it's a little different from walking into a clothing store to buy a jacket and a little longer. Therefore the impression the agent makes has to be one that is individual and one that will last throughout the sales process. This is important because the applicant is a person the agent can use to raise his figures, get a mortgage appointment, earn a commission and sell a house. So, any negative preconceptions the applicant may have need to be quashed as quickly as possible to open the applicant to the other possibilities without hostility.

Tip -It is also important for an agent to make a lasting good impression from start to finish. A good impression may lead to invaluable referrals. So don't be swayed so easily!

The Process

To begin with, an agent needs to make a potential client feel comfortable. When the phone rings, the agent will answer introducing himself and asking you how he may help you, in a polite and courteous manner, a common occurrence with many businesses.

In another instance an applicant may walk directly into the office. Let us take this situation as the example to explain the process.

When a client is walking into the estate agents, the agent will often stand to greet the client, showing a mark of respect, interest and pro-activity. An agent may even rush to the door to open it for you before you enter, particularly in the case of a mother with her children or a pram or an elderly person. In some cases, the agent will even spot the applicant viewing the outside window display and invite them into the office to have a seat and chat about properties they may be interested in.

In both situations, remembering that a **first impression** is key for the estate agent to overcome any preconceived negative views the applicant may have, the estate agent has established that he is there to help you and to provide you with a service. He has also made you feel **important** and **respected** by opening the door for you and making you feel warmly welcomed. The agent will sound bright and alert, irrelevant of his current state of mind, being enthusiastic, courteous and trying to make you feel good about being there. This may in turn serve to inspire a potential buyer to raise his level of interest in what the agent has to say.

What you as a buyer don't know is that you have just entered a fully functional sales environment where the agent has already begun to disarm any preconceived ideas you might have about estate agents with the power of courtesy and good manners and an excellent first impression.

Tip - An agent will often try and make a little conversation to try and find a common ground with you. He may compliment you on a football shirt you are wearing saying he supports the same team or by noticing your car keys talk about a similar vehicle he once had, almost anything he can find out or observe about you that he can use to his advantage. Finding a common ground with you is essential for the agent to build a foundation of trust with you. Making the client feel that you and he are alike in certain areas. Of course this is not the case and the agent will use as many lies as possible to achieve this.

Any good agent will start off by offering you a seat. He will then ask how he may assist you. From this point on it is then his objective to begin to dissect you and to learn whether you are an applicant who may potentially buy and be worth spending time on, or someone just wasting his time. Agents refer to these people as " energy thieves and time-wasters".

He will begin by asking you, " how can I help you today". To which the most common reply if you were looking to buy would be " I'm looking for a house".

The agent has to establish whether you are of potential worth to him or not, whether he can make any money from you and whether he can get you out viewing as soon as possible. In order to do this he will ask you a series of **Open and Quality Questions** that will enable him to get the information he needs from you, as well as getting any other information that may help him in gaining your trust and achieving his goal. This process is known as " whittling down an applicant".

What is a quality question? - A quality question is a question designed to gain as much information as possible from the buyer so the agent knows what they want. A quality question will often produce a quality answer.

What is an open question? - An open question is a question that an agent will ask you that will not limit a buyers responses to a simple yes or no, but instead answers with explanations.

Both types of questions can be used individually or in combination to find out what a buyer is looking for, how long they have been looking and why, as well as finding out the buyer's current position which will help the agent prioritise the buyer.

 These questions also help build an armoury of information for the estate agent that he can use to his advantage. It will help him identify a basic description of the type of property the client wants and needs as well as finding out what a client may have seen.

Tip - Quality and open questions can be used in many variations and in almost any situation you are presented with when dealing with an estate agent. Try and pick up on when they are being used and pick out what kind of information an agent may be trying to get from you. The majority of open and quality questions will be asked in a very subtle and unsuspected way, which is what makes them so effective. They will often begin with words such as what, where, when, why and how?

Tip - An agent will use open and quality questions in many situations to gain as much information as he can, to build a rapport with you. So try and keep your answers focused on what you are looking for, not what he is trying to sell to you, but be always open to suggestions while keeping your main objective in view. You never know!

The estate agent will then try to clarify the current situation of the buyer by asking a few simple and apparently innocent questions that are key to the agent. How soon are you looking to move? What is your current position, could you purchase a property if the right one came along in the next 5 minutes? And what is your price range? All these questions will also help the agent prioritise the applicant in different ways. They will enable him to find out whether the applicant is in a position to move, how quickly they can move and how keen they are to move, as well as helping the estate agent compile a list of properties to offer. (*Another reason an agent may ask you about price is in an attempt to get a mortgage appointment but this will be discussed later on in chapter 5.*) The answers given will also be a good indication to the estate agent as to amount of time needed with that particular applicant.

For example –

If the applicant is a first time buyer with a large deposit, a buyer who has just sold a property, an investor or cash buyer with nothing to sell, they would be in an excellent position to purchase. The agent would then know they are serious about buying and put them into a high priority category.
Similarly if the applicant's house is not on the market but is within the area covered by an agent, it would be an ideal opportunity for the agent to ask for a valuation. This may result in the agent getting two avenues of business from the applicant, a property to sell and an applicant who will be in a strong position to buy. This would also qualify as a high priority client.

On the other hand, if the applicant has a house that needs to be sold first, in another area and is not on the market then, it is not the most powerful buying position and estate agents will very rarely focus too much time on such an applicant. In most cases they would either fall into a low priority category or the estate agent would not contact them after they have left the office, regarding them as " time wasters".

The agent will then ask questions that will help him further whittle down the applicant: -

"What properties have you seen already?" This will tell the agent whether you are actively out viewing with other agents and what he is up against. If the applicant has not seen any other properties, then the agent will try and get that client out viewing as soon as possible. This is done with the intention to stop the applicant seeing any other properties that may be on offer with competing agents and securing the chances of a sale.

" What have you thought of the properties you have viewed already?" This would allow the agent to learn about particular things you have already viewed and make him aware of any obstacles he may need to overcome before offering you the properties he has on his books.

Tip - Estate agents will often mix an element of comedy in with quality and open questions as well as with closes to make you laugh which automatically will put you in a more comfortable frame of mind. So don't find his jokes too funny!

Succeeding Where Other Agents Have Failed

During the process of "whittling down" the estate agent may take the opportunity to excel in areas where his competitors have failed. He may ask the buyer what they thought of the service provided by competing estate agents in the area and whether the applicant had been let down in any way.

If the applicant mentions a previous bad experience, for example one where they had dealt with a competing agent who wasn't helpful or was rude, then the estate agent will automatically know that by increasing his efforts in this area he will gain the favour of the buyers. He will try and help the client as much as possible so that they feel their needs are being catered to. It will also give the impression that the estate agent is not someone who is trying to sell them something but rather someone who is trying to help them achieve what they want. In many situations, people don't only buy a product; they also buy the person selling the product so it is key for the agent to utilise this and any extra information he can use to sell himself as well as the product. We all have a hook and the agent will do his best to find it and once he has, he will use it to increase the level of faith and trust you have in him.

Tip - The agent will often use the failure of others to his advantage with his sales pitch. So try not to give the agent the opportunity. Let him make his impression off his own bat, not the bats of competing agents.

Trick – If the applicant is in a high priority category then the agent will attempt to create an opportunity by which he may increase the amount of time in which he has to build a rapport with that applicant and in turn increase the applicants faith in him. Although estate agents often work against each other in the office, they sometimes join forces in what is called " office assistance". Another agent in the office will offer the applicant a beverage maybe tea or coffee, or a soft drink. This sounds very courteous but this display of good manners is accompanied by an ulterior motive. Not only will a buyer feel more appreciated by the agents but once they have identified the client to be a worthwhile one, the key is to keep them in front of the agent as long as possible. The more time the agent has with the client, the more the opportunity arises to build a stronger rapport, gain trust, make you feel comfortable and sell you other products and services.

The Agent's Approach to What You Want

The Estate agent's approach will change when it comes to finding out what you are looking for in a property. The agent will often only take down limited details of what you are looking for. For example "three bedroom between price range £150,000 and £200,000" is all he may write against your name on the applicant card. He does this because the more specific and detailed an applicant is in describing what he or she is looking for in a property, the more limited the estate agent is in what he offers and the less flexible the buyer will be. Many agents have lost sales by not offering all options available in a particular price range, so it is imperative that they do this and has now become a common rule among many agents.

The agent needs the applicant to be open and flexible on his or her choices. By discussing vaguely what a buyer is looking for in a property the estate agent will be able to offer a much greater number of properties to the buyer and increase his chance of sales based on the viewing to sale ratio. (The agent may also book a viewing for the applicant even if it doesn't match what he or she asked for, the reason for this will be discussed in the next chapter.)

At times you may notice that when you ask an estate agent for details on a particular property or when they call to tell you about a property, they will give you limited information. This is because the agent tries to use mystery to get you out viewing as soon as possible as opposed to talking too much about the properties there and then. Also it serves as a temporary barrier to any negative points that may stop the applicant viewing and by keeping you in the dark the agent can book more properties to view and increase his figures and chances of sale. (However, at times an agent will often use pre-selling of a property to overcome any negative points a property may have.)

An example of this limited information approach would be –

" Jack, I've three houses, all in your price range, all in the area you wanted, I don't want to ruin the surprise by telling you about them now. Will you be free on Tuesday or Wednesday?"

Or

" Jack, I've got a number of properties that are very close to what you want, all I need is one hour of your time for you to have a look at them, will you be free on Tuesday or Wednesday night?"

As mentioned before it is important for an agent to try and make his buyer as flexible as possible in regards to the properties they view. Estate agents will not only offer properties based on what a buyer specifically wants but also very often on what is available in their price range. It is then up to the agent to get them out viewing based on these selections.

Although by now the estate agent has obtained all the information required and has probably built a good rapport through conversation and communication with the applicant, he still has a lot of work to do!

Pre-selling

As we mentioned, once the estate agent has become aware of your buying position, he will select a number of properties that he feels may be roughly what you are looking for and that fall into your price bracket, and he may more often than not begin pre-selling them.

Pre-selling is the way in which an estate agent begins to sell a property before the applicant views it. The intention is to overcome any negatives about the property beforehand so that it prepares the viewer for what they are about to see and they don't become put off by certain features. It also serves to build up any positives that may appeal to the applicant.

It's very simple for an agent to pre-sell the positives; all he has to do is list them. However pre-selling for the negatives is a little trickier. Often the agent will use a tactic called **outweighing** to overcome the negatives. This is achieved by mentioning the negative about the property and then straight after using the word "**But**" followed by a positive point that outweighs the negative aspect of the property, thereby neutralising the negative in the mind of the potential buyer. It can also be used when an agent tries to offer a property or feature to an applicant that may not necessarily appeal to his wants such as a flat instead of a house or a green kitchen instead of a blue one.

For example –

" I have the perfect house for you, however it does have a garden that is a little on the modest side but it's easy to maintain. In addition to that there is a beautiful quiet park right across the street which many residents in the area visit".

Or

" I can appreciate this property has a cosy third bedroom, but it would be ideal for you to use as an office and maybe in the future as a nursery for the baby, with most homes in this price bracket you'll be hard pressed to find one bigger. But on the upside this property is a little more affordable than the others and has much more to offer in regards to condition and decor".

Or

" I know you wanted a house and this is a flat, but for the money you are looking to spend, you get so much more in a flat and the resale value on flats is incredibly high in this area. Not only would you be getting your moneys worth but a great investment opportunity too."

Each pre-sale is unique to the property on offer but agents usually have their points and rebuttals prepared for each. If the agent achieves his goal, he may get you out viewing more properties than you may have originally planned to view, even if they are ones you hadn't considered previously. This will increase the agents' chances of a sale based on the viewing to sale ratio and increase his viewing figures. (But there is a another reason that agents are so keen to get you to view more than just one property or just the one property you specifically asked to view, the reason for this will be revealed in chapter 3.)

Tip - Agents may not necessarily pre-sell you a property in the office. They may ask you to accompany them in their own cars, so that it saves you time and money in petrol, once again trying to put the idea in your head that the agent has your best interests at heart as he tries to do all he can. This will in turn make you even more comfortable and trusting of the agent. However, getting you in his car is a great way of breaking the ice between applicant and agent. He will not only have you in an environment that is completely in his control and from which you can't get away but he will also be able to increase the amount of time spent with you and thereby build a stronger rapport with you. As mentioned before, the longer you are with the agent the more time he has to break you down. Also be careful of ice breaking tools; estate agents will often have cigarettes and chewing gum in their cars, these were great ice breaking tools for even the C.I.A in building contacts, so for an estate agent they are like gold.

Under Promising and Over Delivering

The estate agent will sometimes use another tool found within pre-selling called **under promising and over delivering.** At times the agent will pre-sell the negatives of a property so well that when an applicant actually comes to view the property, it appears much better than the agent originally described it to be. This puts forward to the buyer the impression that the property over delivers in its features, against the description the agent had previously given. The intention here is to make the applicant believe that they are getting more than they originally expected, which would please most of us. This also makes the buyer more accepting of the negatives or other possibilities.

Closing an Applicant for Viewings

Based on all the information the agent has gathered by now it is up to him to get the applicant out viewing, so how does he do it? Well the agent will have to use " closes". We mentioned closes briefly earlier in the book. Now you will see what types of "closes" an agent will use, how and why.

The Assumption Close

The first close an agent may use is the " **assumption close**". The agent in a direct approach uses this close. This close automatically assumes the answer within the question. It directs an applicant to respond with an answer that has been pre-supposed within the question.

For example –

" I hope you don't mind but I've booked you in to see five other properties as well as the one you asked for, we had an hour so I thought it might be beneficial for you to see what else is on the market. I'm sure you'll agree!"

In this example, the estate agent has used the close in an attempt to limit the applicants' response to one already pre-programmed within the question; it also serves his agenda for an increase in viewing figures. By assuming that the applicant wants to see other properties, as well as stating the benefit to the client of doing this he makes it very hard for the applicant to refuse the appointments. Also he has led them to believe that they may actually be losing out on market knowledge that could be essential to decision making by not viewing these extra properties. In addition to this not viewing these properties would also disappoint the owners with whom the appointments have been booked.

(Notice here how the agent also takes advantage of the hour time slot to make the extra bookings so he can increase his viewing figures.)

The "Or" Close

The next close an estate agent may use is known as the **"Or" close**. This is commonly used by estate agents when booking appointments. The objective behind this close is to create a question that already has optional answers built within the question, each of which has a successful result for the estate agent.

For example -

" Will you be available to view this property during the week or at the weekend, evening or daytime?"

Or

" When can I have an hour of your time to view some properties, this afternoon or tomorrow morning?"

The purpose of the "OR" close is to create a barrier against giving a closed and limited response such as yes or no. The agent's intention of asking you a question in the form of the "or close" is for you to respond with one of the already presupposed answers in the question or a similar type of answer, each of which has the same result for the estate agent. It is very similar to attempting to answer A or B on a multiple choice exam, when the only options you've been given is X or Y. Many people will pick one of the answers already in front of them as opposed to creating their own or leaving it blank. This "close" works on a similar sort of psychology.

The Dual Close

The next close an agent may use is called the " **dual close**". The dual close is a combination of the " Or" close and the "assumption" close. It gives the effects of the " OR" and the " assumption close" in one hit. The objective behind it is to put forward two assumed options and also to direct the applicant towards one of the two (both of which are accompanied by their benefits to the client).

For example –

"I've got three perfect properties for you all with a special something and all within your price range, all you have to do is choose one. I hope you don't mind but I arranged all three bookings because I thought you would want to know what else was available to you on the market. All I need to know is when you have an hour free, on Tuesday or Wednesday night? But I really need to know as soon as possible so I can get you in first because my colleague does have some other people interested and properties like this don't come along every day. I would not want you to miss out. So which will it be?"

The estate agent has automatically assumed that it would be in the buyers' best interest to have a look at all three. By not looking at all three the applicant may feel that he would be missing out on key knowledge of the market within which he is looking to purchase. Furthermore the agent has arranged the bookings with the owners on one of two specific evenings limiting the time within which the buyer may view the properties.

(You will also notice the estate agent uses a lot of moral and emotional blackmail. He makes you feel you will be churlish in failing to comply).

Using Fear of Loss and Urgency

In the example above the agent has used two accompanying closes in his sales spiel. These closes are the " **fear of loss close"** and the **" urgency close".** They can both be used in a number of different situations and are particularly effective when closing a buyer into offering on a property.

The **" fear of loss"** close is commonly used to scare a buyer into doing something. The objective is to make the client believe that the opportunity presented is a one off and by not going for it they may lose it altogether.

Here is the same example again -

"I've got three perfect properties for you, all with something to offer, and all within your price range. All you have to do is choose one. I hope you don't mind but I arranged all three bookings because I thought you would want to know what else was available to you on the market. All I need to know is when you have an hour free, on Tuesday or Wednesday night. But I need to know as soon as possible so I can get you in first because **my colleague does have some other people interested and properties like this don't come along every day. I would not want you to miss out.**"

Notice the highlighted section above. As you can see the estate agent makes a special effort to mention that properties like the one he is intending to show the applicant are rare. He tries to plant the idea that if the applicant does not view these properties, other potential buyers may get the property he wants and he will lose out.

The other close used was the " **urgency close**". The urgency close is often incorporated within a question or statement towards an applicant with the intention of planting the notion that the applicant has only a limited period of time in which to make the decision to view. Accompanied with the "fear of loss" it serves a useful purpose when trying to close an applicant into viewing.

For example –

"I've got three perfect properties for you, all with something to offer and all within your price range. All you have to do is choose one. I hope you don't mind but I arranged all three bookings because I thought you would want to know what else was available to you on the market. All I need to know is when you have an hour free, on Tuesday or Wednesday night. **But I need to know within the next hour so I can get you in first especially because my colleague does have some other people interested;** properties like this don't come along every day, I would not want you to lose out."

Notice here again the highlighted section. The estate agent makes reference to the idea of getting you in to view the properties first and making that decision as soon as possible or else you risk losing out. This is essential for the agent to get you viewing as quickly as possible.

Finally, the agent could use the help of two other accompanying closes to clinch the viewing appointment.

The first is the " **best time to buy**" close. It can fortify any of the closes used above. Its objective is to lead a potential buyer to believe that they are getting a **deal** if they go for a property now. It can often be used on 1st time investors or first time buyers who aren't too aware of current market conditions in that area.

For example –

" Jack, you need to see this property, the way the market is right now, what you're getting here is a deal. There aren't too many left of its kind at this price and if you don't buy it, to tell you the truth I certainly won't have a problem selling it to anyone else, but I promised you the first phone call so here it is. The potential of this property will certainly make you a profit; the market growth for this area is huge. Houses in this area usually go for £ 10,000 - £15,000 pounds more, but in this case the owners are in a rush to sell as they are moving abroad, so when's better for you, Tuesday or Wednesday?"

The second is the "**affordability**" close". This close is very similar to the " **best time to buy**" close but again can be highly effective to a buyer who has limited knowledge of the surrounding market, but in this case is also limited on finances. It works based on not only what the buyer wants but also based on what the buyer can afford.

For example –

Jack, we've just had a fantastic property come on the market in your price range. Unfortunately at the budget you have and especially in this area you'll be hard pressed to afford anything more than a two-bed house. But guess what, you're in luck I've found you an affordable three bed. This house is amazing value for money. Not to mention the owner has already found a property and is in a rush to move, so we could probably get an even better price. In my professional opinion it's the best possible house you'll find for what you're looking to spend, either that or unfortunately you'll have to go for a flat, its your choice. All I need to know is which evening is better for you, Tuesday or Wednesday".

Tip - Estate agents will often make their claims based on what you want and then back it up with what they've got and how they feels it will be beneficial to you. So make sure you don't give away too much and see for yourself!

Tip - Always ask the agent if he has seen the property himself. That way he has no excuses even if he lies. If the property isn't what you wanted in the first place you will have good reason to be sceptical in the future when he attempts to get you out viewing again.

Tip - Closes can be used in a number of permutations. What's important is for you to learn to recognise these closes in different types of scenarios and try and adapt the situation to your advantage. Remember an agent will always try and close you on the benefits of a product, so try and highlight the disadvantages of a product to put you in a better bargaining position. And if an agent tells you it has no down side, remember everything has its pros and cons, nothing is 100% perfect.

Tip - Estate agents will sometimes use a gift tactic to whet your appetite about something they are trying to offer you. It seems trivial but has been known to work on occasion. For example, "if you buy this house, you'll not only be getting your dream home but I will even throw in some Ikea vouchers worth £100". Even something as small as cigarettes or gum are used to break you down. Don't accept gifts!

Chapter 3

The Viewing Process

Viewing a property is far from being a complicated process. The majority of people will know the difference between the right and wrong property for them based on what they see, the area it is in and what the property has to offer as far as future potential is concerned. Your estate agent also knows this and will rarely try to sell around these points as he has no control over them. However, he will try to make use of specific methods and tactics that work to his advantage. These methods help him in getting the buyer to move more towards one property than another.

Block Viewings

In the previous chapter we mentioned that estate agents would often try and close an applicant into viewing a number of properties. This is also known as **block viewings**. The estate agent would often justify the block viewings by telling the applicant that it would be beneficial to see these properties, as he would be able to see what else was on offer and gain essential market knowledge. The intention behind this is to make the applicant feel that the agent is looking out for the client's best interests, and this increases the faith the applicant has in the estate agent.

However, as always the agent has his own agenda for arranging these block viewings and its nothing to do with educating the applicant on market conditions. In this chapter we will see why an agent books a number of properties to view and how he uses tried and tested methods that will help him achieve an increase in figures and close an applicant into offering on specific properties an agent has on his books.

Of course no agent can sell you a property that you don't want to buy and in certain situations applicants may find their perfect home on the first viewing. However, if that is not the case then, the agent can use methods that could nudge you towards a specific property. What follows are the different types of methods the agent will use to achieve this throughout the viewing process.

Ways to Book Viewings

The Bracket

The " Bracket" arrangement is one of two approaches the estate agent may use to book a number of properties to view for an applicant. It is very similar to a tactic some politicians use when giving bad news to the country. They would surround a piece of bad news with two benefits. However, the estate agent uses the reverse of this tactic. He will often show an applicant a property not necessarily suitable for the applicant, followed by a fantastic property and then another property that again was not suitable for the applicant. The aim of this approach is to get the applicant comparing the fantastic property to that of the two that are not as appealing to them, and therefore moving the buyer towards the fantastic one and increasing the estate agents chances to close the applicant on that particular one.

5-4-3-2-1 Structure

The " 5-4-3-2-1" arrangement is structured in a way such that the applicant sees a number of properties that each get better as they go along with the best property of them all at the end. It is a build up arrangement. The aim is to get the applicant away from the ideal property they have envisaged and to begin focusing on the properties they are seeing instead. By comparing these ones to each other and with the most saleable property coming at the end, the estate agent's objective is for the applicant to go for the final property based not on what the applicant had envisaged but on what he had just viewed.

Tip – Make sure you do your best to see all the properties that the agent has on his books as well as those that other agents in the area have too. This will give you a greater choice as well as breaking up any structured tactics an agent may try and use. Only when you're happy that you've seen what's available to you should you make an offer.

Viewing the Property

Pre-selling

As mentioned in the previous chapter an agent often uses pre-selling before even showing an applicant a property. It is at this stage in the sales process that pre-selling becomes most effective. An agent will pre-sell the positives and negatives of a property to a buyer before the viewing begins.

For example –

" This is a lovely home, however it does have warm air heating as opposed to gas central heating, but warm air heating is still regarded as a more cost effective and efficient way of heating your home. It is commonly used in countries like Canada where the temperatures hit minus 30 degrees Celsius, so in England it will work a delight".

The intention here is to cushion the applicants for what they are about to see as well as overcoming the negative aspect of the property before they even see it. It also serves to eliminate any resistance the buyer may have to offering over this point by disguising it or outweighing it with a benefit.

Tip- If an agent tries to pre-sell a negative point to you about the property with a benefit, always think of another negative so it makes it more difficult for the agent to come back with a rebuttal and throws him off balance. Try your best to switch it back to what you believe to be right. In this example, you could switch it by saying, "well if it's so effective, then why do most of the houses in the U.K have gas heating?"

Previous Offers

It is quite regular for the estate agent to make an applicant aware that there has been a previous offer on the property, but they can never tell you how much it was. So, why does the agent even bother telling you this in the first place?

Well, making a buyer aware of a previous offer, whether it exists or not has a specific subconscious benefit to an estate agent. By making an applicant aware that there had been a previous offer on the property, the estate shows that the property has generated an interest, and in-turn can generate an interest in the future thus improving the chances of a resale and profit in the future.

However, this raises the question in the potential buyer's head, "why didn't the sale go through if a previous offer was made?"

Although the estate agent will never tell you what was previously offered he overcomes this question by giving you a good reason as to why the sale didn't go through. The reason he gives will never be about the property itself but usually the circumstances surrounding the previous buyer. This may be a number of things ranging from the previous buyer had a property to sell or could not get a mortgage.
However all these reasons the estate agent uses will be a further tactic to nudge the buyer into offering. These reasons are often communicated with the intention of making the new applicant believe that the previous person

lost out on a deal and that you the new buyer could be gaining where they had lost out if they went for this property.

Tip - Don't ask if there have been any previous offers on the property, it has no bearing on your final decision. And if the agent tries to tell you, cut him off and say you're not interested in hearing about any other offers. Don't be afraid to be rude about it if you must!

Trap - Some agents will tell you that a property has been on the market for only a short amount of time. The benefit to the agent here is that it gives the applicant the belief that they are getting first choice. This is essential if they want to offer before another applicant. In particular, if the agent has mentioned the previous offer and given the reason why the buyer lost out, it will further strengthen the idea that they are profiting where someone has previously lost out. The other reason is to keep an applicant from finding out if that property has been sitting stagnant on the market for months and not been sold, which indicates one of two things, either the price is too high or there is something wrong with the property. Also look out for minor details on the pictures, such as leaves on the floor in summer which will indicate how long a property may have been on the market.

Selling During the Viewing - The Demonstration

When buying a product many of us are used to seeing a demonstration before we purchase. The estate agent does a similar thing when showing you a property and as with other salespersons it is up to the estate agent to sell all the benefits and sell around the negatives. Selling the benefits of a house is quite a simple thing, it's something that many applicants can see without the commentary of the agent.

However selling around the negatives is often a little more tricky. So how does an estate agent do this?

To begin with, the agent has already pre-sold certain elements of the property to prepare you for what you are about to see. However he fortifies this with the way in which he describes the property and its features during the viewing. Estate agents have a few certain angles to sell common features of many houses whilst conducting a viewing. These are as follows.

1. The agent will often plan out each viewing beforehand knowing what features to highlight about the property.

2. The agent will always show you the best features of the property first. They do this because it is often much harder for an applicant to make raise negative points about the property if they have already been impressed by its positives.

3. The agent will always present a small room by walking into the furthest corner of it and then sell its features to the applicant. This is in an attempt to create the illusion that the room is larger than it seems.

4. The agent will introduce the applicants to the owners. This allows the applicants and vendors to build a basic rapport. If the applicant likes the vendors then they are more likely to be interested in the house (remembering that people also buy people not just the product). However, this can also work against the estate agent, so it is important that he govern the contact between the vendors and applicants whilst maintaining a comfortable atmosphere in which to conduct the viewing.

5. The estate agent will often use angled words to describe a property. For example, a bedroom will be "cosy" instead of small, a garden will be "easy to

maintain" instead of a concrete patio, a garage will be a " good extra storage area" instead of too small to fit your car.

Tip - After the agent has finished showing you the property ask to look around again. Split up and look in different rooms if you're a couple. This way the agent will be divided between you and he will have already used his sales pitch the first time around. This will leave him with little to say and you will be able to view the property again without any running influential commentary and you can make a more independent and informed decision.

Tip- When you are on the viewing make sure you view the property properly, don't just breeze about it following the estate agent around and taking his word from a distance. Be nosey and ask lots of questions, " why are there so many cracks in the wall?" Remember this is your future home, if you're not going to check it yourself then who will? Of course failing that you can opt for a more detailed survey of the property, a homebuyers report or a full structural survey which will even go as far as soil pH examination. However both these options tend to be much more expensive!

Emotion Spotting

Emotions play an important role when it comes to purchasing a property, or a number of products for that matter. Companies spend hundreds of thousands of pounds a year on advertising their products so that we as buyers associate positive feelings to buying certain products.

In a very similar way the estate agent is also aware that the emotions you associate with a property have great influence on your decision to buy a property. After all, for many of us buying a house will be one of the largest and most expensive investments we ever make and in turn will have a massive amount of emotion attached to it. We as buyers need to be sure that we are happy with what we are buying.

Therefore, it is essential for the estate agent to be able to spot the different emotions a buyer displays towards a property. There are two reasons for this. The first is to pick up on any negative feelings towards the property; this will make the estate agent aware of anything you may not like and allow him to start building up a rebuttal or method to sell around the angle he has to overcome.

For example, if you react to a small garden during a viewing or make a comment such as " the gardens a bit small". The agent will automatically know in his head that this is a point that will need to be sold around when trying to close the buyer for an offer. He may respond with something along the lines of, " well it's easy to maintain" or " with the park across the road, the size of the gardens isn't really an issue in this area".

The second is to see what positive emotions you may display towards the property. By knowing this the agent will know what he can use as his **bargaining chips** when it comes to closing you on the property and negotiating the price. If you react in a positive way to the size of a property then the agent will know that this will be something he can use as a bargaining chip when closing you. He may also try to use it to outweigh a negative aspect of the property, like a small garden.

For example -

" I can see you like the house. It is a fantastic sized property for the price. Houses of this size rarely come on the market at this price, especially in an area as exclusive as this. Usually I'd offer it to one of my investors but I told you I would give you priority so I'm keeping my promise to you. In my opinion, you would be losing out if you didn't buy this house. But that's just my opinion. I know it has a garden that is not as big as what you may be used to, but with the extra space you're getting in the house I'm sure you can convert one of the rooms into a playroom for the kids. There is also a huge park only 5 minutes' walk from here, and I think that's why the gardens in this area are not as big as you would expect. Most people take their kids to the park. Its quite a close community so it serves as a nice little social distraction too and a great way for the kids to make some friends. But I do have to tell you that my colleague just called me and told me he has another interested party looking to view this property. Now I'm not saying they're going to buy it, but if they make an offer then you may lose your chance to buy it".

Tip - Try not to make the estate agent aware of your excitement towards a property. Keep a cool head during a viewing and remember that you still have to make an offer and negotiate a price. Don't give the agent any extra chips in his stack to bargain with. Keep your cards to yourself and make it harder for the agent to call your bluff and take your money.

Closing the Applicant into an Offer

In the previous chapter you were introduced to certain types of closes the estate agent could use to get you out viewing. In a similar way estate agents will use different closes to try and nudge you into offering on a property. Once the agent has shown you the properties and assessed your emotions he will pick an appropriate close to suit the situation.

The " Other Buyer" Close

This close is the most commonly used by an estate agent at the end of a viewing when attempting to get an offer out of the potential buyer! It takes advantage of the positive emotions the applicant may have displayed towards a property during the course of the viewing. (This could be anything from an elevated level of excitement, a change in physiology (i.e. positive facial expressions) or words and phrases used by you during the viewing). Upon identifying the presence of these emotions the estate agent will then introduce the idea of another interested party or **other buyer** to scare you into offering. The agent combines the "other buyer "close with a "fear of loss" and the "urgency" close to get the buyer to offer. The agent knows that if you like this property yet do not offer then, you will be torn apart by the dilemma of " what if I lose it to another buyer, what if nothing better comes along?" or " if I don't offer, what will it cost me?" Therefore the estate agent promotes the idea that the only way to secure the property and stop any other viewings occurring is to offer as soon as possible, secure your position and increase your chances of getting the property before someone else.

For example –

" I know you like the property and in an ideal world any body would want to take their time to make a decision when it comes to investing in your family's future home. But, I do have to tell you there is another interested party and if you want this property, I need to know by 9am tomorrow morning because after that I cant hold off anybody else from offering on it."

Or

" My colleague in the office has another viewing on this property straight after we leave and I don't want you to lose out, so if you want it, you have to make an offer because that's the only way I can stop his viewing going ahead. And as you can see it is a fantastic property, it's ideal for you and you've told me its just what you're looking for, so I wouldn't want you to lose out".

Office Assistance

Further to strengthen the idea of a third party, the estate agent may use a different form of office assistance. Once the estate agent has identified any positive emotions he may send a text message to another colleague in his office or arrange a certain time for the office to call his mobile phone or the vendor's house.

Upon receiving this so-called unexpected phone call the estate agent will put on a small performance in front of the applicant. The message communicated from the agent to the buyer about the phone call would be, " my office has just called me and told me there is another buyer interested in this particular property and they want to view it as soon as possible". Of course we're not stupid, and we're often aware of such tactics. However, the intention of the estate agent is not only to try and fool you with the idea of another buyer alone. It is his intention to put in your head the question" what if there is another buyer, what if he's telling the truth?" As you can imagine this tactic can be quite effective at this level, especially if you've fallen in love with the house. The agent could also strengthen the effects of this tactic if he had a viewing just before you, or there was double booking where he could play one buyer off against the other.

For example –

" I do have to tell you that my colleague just called me and told me he has another interested party looking to view this property. Now I'm not saying they're going to buy it, but if they make an offer then you may lose your chance to buy it. If you offer now I can call him and tell him not to let the viewing go ahead as the property is under negotiation ".

Or

" My colleague has just called and told me that the people who viewed the property just before you have just called the office to find out if the house is sold. I told my colleague that I would call him back in 5 minutes and let him know whether you have offered and if he should tell the other couple that it is gone. We're not in the business of going into Dutch Auctions so I would prefer to give you guys priority as I've been dealing with you longer. If you offer now I can secure your chances and hold off other buyers. So what shall I tell him?"

Evidently the psychology behind this approach is to scare the buyer into believing they will lose the property, but by offering now they will secure their position and not lose the property. Hence they have no choice but to offer.

Key Tip - You must remember for all I have mentioned above and throughout the buying process that failure to communicate all offers to the vendor before the point of exchange is illegal. By law all offers made must be put forward to the owner up until contracts are exchanged; until that point the property is on the still market. This cannot be decided by the estate agent; however, in some cases, it has been known to happen. Therefore do not feel pressured into having to make an offer there and then. You have time to make a decision, so don't feel pressured. Even if the agent has told you it has been sold after you viewed it and that he can't communicate your offer, you can still make the vendor aware directly by dropping a note or knocking on their door. However, waiting too long to communicate your offer may also put you at a disadvantage. Firstly the owner may not feel you were serious about the property, otherwise you would have offered before and may therefore reject your offer. Secondly the owner may not deal with you out of courtesy to their current buyer. Or thirdly you

may end up in a Dutch auction over the property. Therefore, although I recommend you to take the time to make the right decision, I wouldn't recommend you take longer than 24 hours. And don't be phased or feel forced into making a decision straight after a viewing, even if the agent tries to scare and close you with the idea of another buyer. You can still offer if you've viewed it, up until the point of exchange, and follow up on that offer by contacting the owner directly if you feel the agent has failed to do so.

Accompanying Closes

Although the " other buyer" close is the most commonly used by the estate agent, the agent may also use a number of accompanying closes to fortify any other closes he has used when trying to get an applicant to offer.

The Companion Close

The companion close is designed to focus on particular members of a couple or group that are buying. It is often used when an agent sees that one of the people viewing is more interested and focuses his sales pitch on that person. The aim is to rely on the more interested party to convince the less interested party of the benefits of purchasing the property, but in their own private time later on without feeling pressured by an estate agent.

For example - Imagine yourself in this situation!

Mrs.X loves the property because it's all she ever wanted. However Mr.X is more sceptical. The estate agent will focus his energy on reinforcing the positive aspects to Mrs.X so that she will have more ammunition with which to convince Mr.X later in the day, away from the pressures of the agent.

The agent may also focus on personalised information to achieve this goal; for example, highlighting a particular benefit of the property that may appeal to Mrs.X. This could be a number of things, such as proximity to local primary schools and safety of the area. Alternatively it could work in reverse for Mr.X. The agent could highlight proximity to the local golf course or a social venue that may appeal to his nature.

Tip- In this situation again keep a cool head. Don't give away too much to the agent or he will use it against you. Discuss things with your partner, relation or friend in your own time. Don't let the agent single you out! And furthermore build a list of pros and cons for yourself to keep a balanced view, then you will both be able to see the property objectively.

Adjournment Close

The adjournment close is designed to give a buyer time to think. It is often used when an agent is unsure as to how serious a buyer is. In order to make a strong sale the estate agent needs to be sure that a buyer has strong enough reasons to buy the property. This is very simply because at times a sale made quickly can be a sale lost quickly.

In an earlier example the estate agent used the words, " I need to know by 9am tomorrow morning". This gives the buyer enough time to make a solid decision and up until that time the estate agent can afford to wait for a decision before recommencing viewing.

A positive response from the buyer after the adjournment period is often enough to give the estate agent the confidence that this buyer has given serious thought and formed enough reasons to support his decision to purchase. In turn it provides a sense of security for the agent and more often than not a buyer is less likely to change his mind or pull out of the sale.

Tip - This close is actually beneficial to you both, agent and buyer. Use the time the agent gives you wisely, to make your decision. This will save fewer headaches for all parties involved later. Although all offers must be communicated up until the point of exchange, don't take too long or it could work against you, as I mentioned previously.

Affordability Close

The " affordability" close as mentioned in the previous chapter can be varied to support the closing of a sale. It is particularly useful when the buyer has limited knowledge of the surrounding market. The agent can use this opportunity to direct the buyer into believing that this property is the best they can afford, based on their price range.

For example –

" Well we've seen five properties today and Jack, at the price you're looking to buy at, mark my words you can't get a better house than this. I know it needs a little work, but its just cosmetic. I know you're limited to a purchase price of £180,000 and this is on the market for £190,000 but I'll speak to the owner and tell him you're a good buyer; he's in a rush to sell, so we should be able to get him down to £180,000. Otherwise you'll have to settle for something else like a flat, and to tell you the truth, deals like this don't come along very often, and house prices aren't getting any lower, so you don't want to be in a position where you can't afford anything at all. But if you get this property at the right price, you'll make money, get on the property ladder and when you come to sell it on, you'll have a lot more options to choose from, thanks to the money you'll make from this one. But for now it's the best you're going to get at the price you're looking at".

As you can see, the estate agent has limited the options the buyer has in offering, based on what he can afford, by making the buyer feel that he is getting a good deal for the price he is paying on this property. And by making him believe that he can't get better for the price he is looking to buy at, the estate agent closes the gap for the buyer to offer. He puts the idea in the buyer's mind, that if he does not offer on this property, he wont be able to afford another and may lose out altogether on being able to climb onto the property ladder.

Tip - Research the market you're about to buy in. See what other agents have to offer before you feel forced into making a decision after viewing only a few properties with one or two agents. Make sure you don't miss a deal just because they have convinced you that there is nothing else you can afford.

"Best Time to Buy" Close

Another close used by the estate agent is the " best time to buy" close; again this is an accompanying close to fortify any closes already made. It is to reassure a buyer that they are getting a deal if they purchase now, it is very good for 1st time investors or first time buyers who aren't too aware of current market conditions in that area.

For example –

" The way the market is right now it is the best time to buy; what you're getting here is a deal. There aren't too many left of its kind at this price and if you don't buy it, I certainly won't have a problem selling it to anyone else. The potential of this property will certainly make you a profit; the market growth for this area is huge. Houses in this area usually go for £ 10,000 - £15,000 pounds more, but, in this case, the owners are in a rush to sell, as they are moving abroad. So if you want to benefit then I suggest you offer now; as I said before it's the best time to buy, otherwise you may lose it and any potential earnings you could gain in the future ".

Tip – Once again research your market. There are a number of web sites that may be helpful or the local council will have information on property growth etc. failing that you can always obtain a title register from the land registry for a fee of about £3 or £4. This will tell you precisely what the property sold for previously, and you can do your sums on growth based on that. This will let you know whether the agent is telling you facts or just trying to sell you ideas.

Balance Sheet close

The " balance-sheet" close is used by the estate agent to measure up the pros and cons of each of the properties viewed and play one off against the other. He can also do this with a single viewing, playing off the pros and cons of the property within itself although this is a little trickier. Nonetheless the idea is the same. By the time the agent has finished listing the pros and cons, the pros must outweigh the cons enough for a buyer to be nudged towards the property.

For example –

" The first house had a small garden, the second wasn't the greatest area, the third was outside the school catchment area, the fourth was a bit small and as you can see this one has the opposite of all those things, and so much more to offer. It's newly refurbished, a huge garden, lovely living space, it's just come on the market so you're the first to see it, it's a lovely quiet area and within minutes walking distance to the two best schools in the area, so it will be safer for the kids. Crime rates are the lowest in the area, near enough nil. And the price, its certainly well within your budget".

Or

" The house is in need of a new gas central heating system, as well some decorating work. But, it's a huge property, in a good size plot, with great potential. And at the price it is being offered at, it's a deal as it is, and I'm sure you'll be able to get a few thousand off it as well during negotiation; what have you got to lose? ."

Tip - By listing all the pros and cons for you, the agent is intending to obviate your need to do so. By making you believe he has listed all the pros and cons, he hopes to make you see only what he wants you to see, in the hope that you will fail to form your own ideas about the property. So, go home, take out a sheet of paper and list them for yourself, and don't be afraid to call the agent to fill in any missing bits of information or things you don't remember. And if it's something that you require proof of, get it! Don't take the agent's word that the lease on a flat is 150 years, make sure you get him to check with the owner. Although your solicitor will bring up such points, its wise for you to do your best to find out certain information first, otherwise you'll end up spending money unnecessarily.

The Doubt Close

The " doubt" close is a type of reverse psychology close. Taking into consideration that few estate agents hold psychology degrees, their use of this close is minimal but nonetheless at times effective. Here the estate agent will show you that he has doubt in a particular aspect of a property or the property itself and then leave room for you to disagree with him. This is so that the buyer creates his own reasons to accept this negative aspect and see it as a minor detail. At the same time this response makes it easier for the estate agent to close the buyer about the negatives of the property as well as having less objections to overcome, thus leaving space that can be filled with more reasons to buy.

For example – Imagine yourself in this situation

Agent – " well it is a fantastic property John, it's a lovely location, good condition and a good price, but I don't think it's the one for you".

Buyer - " why do you say that?"

Agent – " even though it's a beautiful house, I don't like the third bedroom, I think it's a little small for what you want".

Buyer – " yeah I agree with you, it is a bit small but that's a small point when compared to the rest of the house. At the end of the day it is a third bedroom, and the third bedroom is always the smallest one, so I'll have to assume that's something that's going to be in every property I look at ".

Agent: " Well I'm glad you can say that John, I wish my other buyers were as open-minded as you".

Tip - When you feel the agent is trying to use this psychology, agree with him. This will throw him off balance. His intention is for you to sell around the negative yourself. By agreeing with him you give him one more obstacle to overcome, and what's more the shock will make it harder for him to be creative and come up with a good response or rebuttal.

Quality Close

With the " quality" close the estate agent will bring all the positives of a property together and put them forward to you with the idea that all things considered, this is a one of a kind property.

For example –

"John, the current owner of this property is in the building trade. As you can see he has put a lot of time and effort into every aspect of this property. From the granite worktops in the kitchen to the marble flooring in the bathroom, the workmanship is flawless. It is in a fantastic condition, in a good location, the schools here are among some of the best in the area, so it's beneficial for the children too. It's a good size and I don't have to tell you that you won't have a problem selling it again. Most important of all, it's on at a price that is slightly under market value for a property of this quality, because he's found another project to undertake and needs to sell this as quickly as possible. But I do have to tell you that there is another viewing that's going to take place tonight at 6pm. I'm not saying they will buy it, but I like you John and I wouldn't want you to risk losing out. I'm sure you'll agree, this property is one of a kind and a real find, that's why I'm giving you priority here".

Tip - If the house is of good quality, its something you'll be able to see for yourself. If you cant see it, then don't just take the agent's word for it, and make sure you're happy with what you see, regardless!

In conclusion, all these closes can be used individually or as supports to fortify the " other buyer" close. All this accompanied by a " fear of loss" and an element of "urgency" is often extremely effective and serves well to nudge a buyer into the offer position. So, be aware of their use, recognise them and watch out for the different variations in which they may be used.

Tip - Surveyors will often assess the value of a property for a lender and down-value a property if they feel that the purchase price is too high. However, it is still a great concern for many of us that we may end up paying over the odds for a property that has been over-valued. In

some cases, buyers have been known to pay tens of thousands extra than what a property is worth. However there is a way you can find out if you're paying over the odds. You can contact the land registry or go on their web site and find out what the property had sold for previously, by buying its Title Register, there is a small charge of about £3, which is a small price to pay when you could be paying thousands more. Then find out what market growth is in that area, as well as comparing the price to surrounding properties on the market. Then do your sums and see if you're paying tens of thousands extra for a coat of paint and a year's growth that's only really a couple of thousand. Although, surveyors will do this on behalf of the mortgage lender, some estate agents have been known to corrupt information that they pass on to surveyors. So for that extra peace of mind, this is an effective method.

Tip- By far the best technique to throw an agent off during a viewing is silence. It will stop the agent from knowing what you're thinking and he will not know what angle to take with you when selling. And if the agent starts asking you questions, keep your responses limited. Use silence as your tactic and always keep cool!

Chapter 4

Negotiating the Price- The Deal

Negotiating the price is very much a cat and mouse game, and there isn't much that can be said about it. Each estate agent has different ways of communicating offers between buyers and sellers and negotiating the price. However, they all use a few similar tactics.

The Time Game

The time game is a good way for the estate agent to keep a buyer walking on eggshells when it comes to negotiating the price. Is it intended to keep the buyer waiting for a response as to whether their offer has been accepted or not.

For example –

Agent: " Hi John, I've called the owners but they weren't home so I've left them a message. So when they call me back, Ill put your offer forward and see what they say".

Or

Agent: " Hi John, I've spoken to the owner, he's really happy that you offered, but he would like to think about it".

Or

Agent: " Hi John I've spoken to the owner of the property, he's really happy you decided to offer, but he would like to speak to his wife before making any decisions. Unfortunately she's at work at the moment, so as soon as they've called me back, Ill let you know".

The longer the agent can keep a buyer hanging, the more open to options they become. This is because the buyer will constantly be plagued by the dilemma; " Did we offer enough? Should we offer a bit more?" and " what if someone offers more and we lose it" or " What if they don't accept our offer?" The estate agent will almost always use this to his advantage when the buyer expresses a genuine interest in a property. The longer the buyer waits for a response, the more they will worry that they may lose the property. As a result of this the buyer then begins to consider other options; for the most part these considerations would usually fall into two categories, an increase in their original offer and an increase in their intended target purchase price for that property.

In addition to this, the time element is also intended to turn your wants into needs. People will usually pay more money for something they need as opposed to something they want. If you like the property, then the fear that you may lose it accompanied with all the above will certainly have a bearing on what you're willing to offer, or at least improve the chances of your increasing your offer.

The Silent Close

The second is the "Silent " close. Nearly every sales person will use this close at one point or another in their careers. But with an estate agent it is the most commonly used close when negotiating the price.

The "silent" close is a closing technique by which a salesperson presents a product to a buyer and then deliberately stops talking. The aim is to back the buyer into a corner with silence so that they are subconsciously forced to respond. The response will allow the agent to assess how willing the buyer is to go up in price for the property and how much pressure needs to be applied on the buyer in order to get them to increase their offer based on their reaction. Thereby giving the agent the upper hand in the negociation.

The estate agent will often use the "silent" close when going back to the buyer with the owners' response to the offer. It can sometimes be accompanied with gratitude and compliment to cushion the buyer into offering a higher price the second time around. (This is also where the introduction of the buyer to the owner can come in handy, as mentioned in the chapter 3. The agent can use the introduction between the two as an assist for his close).

For example –

Agent – " hi John, I've spoken to the owner about your offer; they really liked you when you came to view the property and said they're happy that their home could be going to someone like you. But, they would like a little more ...Silent Close!

Buyer: "Well, how much more do they want?"

Agent: " They didn't give me an exact figure but we're not too far away, you can try another offer and Ill go back to them with it, how much more would you consider going up to and maybe I can put that forward on your behalf?"...
Silent Close

As you can see, the agent stops deliberately at pre-planned points to leave the buyer to come back with a response that leans toward the notion of a higher offer.

The Compliment Close

Next is the "compliment" close. This is an assisting close that the agent may use alongside the silent close. The aim of this close is to flatter the buyer into submission. In the previous example the estate agent called the buyer and said, *", they really liked you when you came to view the property and said they're happy that their home could be going to someone like you"*. This is a perfect example of the " compliment" close. The agent highlights that the owners want the client to buy the property as he is so wonderful and hold him in higher regard than the other people who came to view the property. This puts the buyers in a much more positive frame of mind and increases their emotional associations towards the property and the vendors, building an illusory relationship between the two parties. This could then serve to increase the chances of a higher offer and on the other side form an element of guilt on the buyers' part should they fail to achieve the target price or not purchase the property.

The estate agent will almost always use one or a combination of these tactics and closes and in different variations to try and influence a greater purchase price. So make sure you recognise them! If he has gained your trust then it is very easy for you to assume he is working in your best interests and working to get you the property you want for the best possible price. But, you have to remember throughout this whole process **the estate agent works in the best interests of the vendor and not the buyer**. It is the estate agent's aim to achieve the highest possible purchase price for the owner as it will increase his level of commission and earn him more money, not to get the buyer the best possible price. Even if your agent is trustworthy always remember that, in this situation, the agent is certainly not working in your best interests, but in the vendors` best interests, because they are the ones that pay him, not you!

Tip –Always remind the agent of how good a buyer you are. If you throw enough mud at a wall, some of it will stick. By constantly reminding the agent of your buying position and how it may be beneficial to the sale, the more likely the agent is to use it when discussing the price with the owner. By doing this, the owner will also become aware of your situation and begin to open to the idea of a solid buyer. The awareness of a solid buyer can play a key role in negotiating the price. The owner would then be faced with his own dilemma and a choice.

" Would I rather sell my house to someone who may pull out of the sale a few weeks later or sell it for a thousand pounds less to someone that is more likely to go through with the sale? Or " if I don't take this buyer now, will I get another?" Most of us will rather go with the solid buyer and less paracetamol. Remember the owner has the final say, not the agent, the agent is just a middle- man, so keep reminding him. It can be your "good buyer" and "repetitions" close on the agent.

Gazumping

Once you have agreed an offer and are happy with a purchase price you may still be in danger of losing the property. **Gazumping** is a word that has caused many of us unnecessary anxiety when purchasing a property. **Gazumping** occurs when a vendor after having accepted an offer from one party, sells it to someone else for a higher price. However the estate agent can also play his role in the Gazumping process.

Gazumping can also occur when an estate agent runs multiple buyers on a property, i.e. two or more offers on a property and tries to push the sale on both of them simultaneously. He keeps the other buyers in the shadows so that if the original buyer pulls out of the sale, he has a back-up and secures his paycheque. However, it usually becomes a race to see which buyer is the more serious and with which the sale will progress quicker. (This is because an agent only gets paid once the sale has gone through, so it is in his best interests to run with the buyer who can complete more quickly). Unfortunately it's often the case where both buyers are serious and love the property, but the agent has to let one of them go. Hence the term "Gazumped".

Of course, the agent will for the most part make out that this isn't his fault. He will make an excuse saying it was by choice of the owner and that he was powerless to stop it, or that they've decided not to sell. (However, most of us usually put two and two together, especially when the sold board is erected).

By shifting the blame, the agent attempts to maintain what little faith the gazumped buyer may have left in him and keep a buyer that is in a red-hot position to proceed on another property. Now, all the agent needs to do is find the applicant another property, and he gets another sale.

Tips on How to Avoid Gazumping

Tip - As mentioned in the previous chapter, all offers must be communicated to the vendor by law. If you are worried that the agent hasn't communicated your offer to the owner and are concerned about Gazumping then you can always knock on the vendors' door or drop a note through the letterbox. This note could say something along the lines of " hi, we were just passing your house again and wanted to say we love it so much, and we hope you're interested in our offer". Make sure you put your name and telephone numbers in case the owner decides to contact you about the offer that they never heard about from the agent.

Tip - Another good way for the buyer to secure his purchase is to ask the agent to view the property again as you want to take some measurements, once you go to do that, have a word with the owner in regards to the offer or deal negotiated.

Tip - You can also get a friend to call up the estate agents about the property you have agreed to purchase and see if the agent is still marketing that property. If the agent is still getting viewings with other buyers, then it is possible you may end up being Gazumped in the future. If this is the case, confront the estate agent and catch him out! And in the meantime start looking at other properties, just in case.

Tip - Try and swap phone numbers with the owners once you have agreed a deal. Use the excuse that you want to discuss the sale of furniture or something along those lines. This will ensure you constant communication between yourself and the vendor and minimise the chances of being gazumped.

Tip - You can now purchase a legitimate anti-gazumping agreement for as little as £5 off the Internet. This agreement is a legal contract between the seller and purchasers that will stop the seller dealing with any other parties for an exclusive period of time, however after this time period has expired the seller is free to sell to another party.

Chapter 5

Estate Agency and Mortgages

Brokers – Why They are in Agent's Offices and What are the Benefits to the Advisor?

House buying and mortgages are inextricably linked. This is why you will often find agents and advisors co-operating. However financial services play a vital role within many estate agent offices when it comes to buying or selling a home. In the previous chapters we made reference to estate agents and financial appointments. In this chapter we will discuss the role a financial advisor plays within the estate agent's, how the agency benefits, and the issues that buyers need to be aware of. The objective in this chapter is not to discuss the workings of a financial advisor, but rather to focus on the way in which agents use advisors to achieve their goals.

(NB. The financial service authority for the majority of their business regulates financial advisors, not the estate agency.)

The two main benefits to the estate agency itself are: -

1. **Money** – any commission earned by a financial advisor (via mortgage and/or related insurance policies or products) will more often than not be shared between the financial advisor and the introducing estate agency.

For example –

a typical commission split would be 2/3 retained by the advisor, and 1/3 going to the estate agency. If a mortgage advisor arranged a £200,000 mortgage and also arranges some sort of mortgage protection package for the buyer,

The commission generated from such a sale could potentially amount to a £2000-£3000 commission split as mentioned above.

2. **Regulation of the sale** – Having an in-house advisor arrange a mortgage for a potential buyer ensures that the estate agent has a greater control over the progression of the sale, primarily being able to liase with the advisor on a frequent basis to establish progress, tackle any issues as they arise (e.g. a negative property valuation) and cement a more secure house purchase. More often than not, buyers are less likely to pull out of a purchase if they have arranged their mortgage via the same office they are buying through. The financial advisor also plays a key role in establishing the "quality" or otherwise of an applicant at first registration stage and before an applicant makes a genuine offer. This is primarily due to the fact that many property buyers especially those buying for the first time will not have sought mortgage advice prior to actually looking for a property.

Apart from the general benefits mentioned to the agency, the negotiator can also gain financially and achieve a higher level of figures in relation to performance targets. Many estate agency companies pay their negotiating staff either a flat fee or a percentage of commission generated from the mortgage lead the estate agent has provided.

The Estate Agents Agenda

In all cases an estate agent needs to clarify a buyer's financial position. The reason for this is that no estate agent wants to be out of the office showing a house to a person who can't afford it, when there could be a more profitable buyer who has just walked into the office. Furthermore this potentially beneficial client could end up sitting with the estate agents colleague. It's a risk very few agents like to take as they might lose out on business for themselves. In order to clarify your financial position the agent may ask you a series of financially based questions.

For example - "Have you arranged a mortgage yet?" or who is your mortgage arranged with?" or " have you got a deposit in place?" or " do you have an agreement in principal or AIP?" or " how have you come to the figure you are planning to purchase at?"

There is nothing wrong with answering these questions, but as always the agent does have another agenda in place as well as learning about your financial position. The agent will try and close you into seeing his financial advisor. This is because a quality appointment alone can earn him a commission regardless of whether the financial advisor gets the business. So the agent's objective is to get you financially qualified and to get **"bums on seats"**.

Agents do not sell any financial products themselves, legally they are not allowed to and if you ever came across an estate agent that did then I suggest you seriously reconsider taking any of his advice. However they do sell the benefits of seeing their advisor. Some applicants may have already seen a financial advisor and some not. Either way it is irrelevant to the agent. Because the estate agency earns commission from the mortgage arrangements, the estate agent is often under pressure to push for an appointment throughout the sales process.

However if an agent fails to secure an appointment at the registration stage, he will often wait until he has gained your trust before he tries to close you a second time. The agent will try and secure this trust by giving you the impression that he can save you money through offering you access to in-house mortgage advice and special limited deals. (In some cases agents have even closed outside financial advisors into seeing their advisor).

Regardless of who you are, whether you are looking to re-mortgage your property, buying or selling a home, an agent will always attempt to highlight certain points beneficial to you in seeing his financial advisor. This is not only to help convince you and gain your trust by making you believe that he is working in your best interest but also because it's in his.

Once the agent feels he has educated or intrigued you on the possibilities of your saving more money, he will then use closes to book you in for an appointment.

The closes the agent uses are the same as those used when closing an applicant into viewing a property. In this section these closes have been varied to show how they can be used when booking financial appointments. The underlying approach for each close is the same and for many this section will serve as a refresher to what you have learnt already in **chapter 2**. The closes used are as follows:

The Assumption Close

The first close an agent might use on you is a variation of the " assumption close". It is used with a direct and focused approach like a darts player going for the bulls-eye. This close automatically assumes the answer within the question the agent has asked or statement he has made.

For example -

" I hope you don't mind but I booked you in to see our financial advisor to see if we can save you some money, I'm sure that's something you'd be interested in."

By using this close, the estate agent will limit your responses to one already pre-programmed within the question or statement accompanied by its benefit. In this case the reference to a pre-booked appointment that will save the client money assists the objective of the agent to attain an appointment to see his in house financial representative. By making the assumption for you and with it giving you the benefit of the decision he has made for you, the agent makes it very hard for you to refuse the appointment. To refuse the appointment would make the client think that he may actually be losing out on something if he doesn't go along with what the agent has said, but by going along with what the agent has said he has only to gain and nothing to lose. Furthermore this close is one that can rarely be responded to with a closed answer such as no. Therefore the buyer's answer will tend to be one that leans toward the agent's objective or one which the agent will be able to sell around.

The Or Close

To further increase the chances of getting this appointment the agent may use another close known as The "Or" close. It is a little different from the " assumption close" in that it gives you the option of two answers as opposed to a pre-programmed answer like in the " assumption close". This is a very common close used by estate agents in booking appointments. The idea of this close is to create a question that already has two or more answers built in it and put it forward to the client.

For example –

" Will you be free to see my financial advisor, on Tuesday or Wednesday?"

The estate agent will often use the "Or" close to ask a question because it is already creating a psychological barrier against answering a simple yes or no. The agent knows that by asking you this question you are more likely to go with one of the already pre – programmed answers within the question or a similar type of answer, each of which has the same result for the Estate agent.

To put it simply, you wouldn't answer a multiple-choice question with Q, when the only answers to choose from were A, B, or C.

The majority will pick one of the answers already in front of them as opposed to creating their own. This "close" works on a similar sort of psychology.

The Dual Close

However there is still a tactic that the estate agent may use to increase his chances of getting this appointment threefold. And that is by combining the two closes already mentioned above. The combination of the " assumption" close and the "Or" close, comes together to create a potent close known as the " Dual Close". This close can be used very much like the previous two closes in a number of different situations and variations.

It gives the effects of the " Or" and the "assumption" close in one hit. Not only will a client be limited in his or her responses, but also they are directed to one of the two answers pre-supposed by the estate agent. This close gives the person being closed, the impression that they only have two options to choose from whilst in reality they are really falling into the trap of the estate agent, as each answer will have a positive result for him. Furthermore a buyer cannot answer yes or no to this type of close as people in this situation would often much rather take one of the options put in front of them as opposed to creating their own answer. It's a lot easier and in some cases people even feel that they would embarrass themselves if they argued another point.

For example –

" Hi John, its Layla! My financial advisor has just told me about the latest rates offered and a new mortgage deal that has just come out. Now, I know as well as you do that moving house isn't cheap so maybe this will save you a little bit extra money. If its not better than the deal you've already got then you'll know you've got the best deal and if it is, then you can buy me lunch with extra money you save, (*ha ha ha*). At least you'll know either way. Let's put it this way, you've got nothing to lose and it costs you nothing. But my advisor has told me he can only offer it to the first three clients and I've saved you a slot, so I need to know what's better for you, Monday evening or Tuesday? He can even do a home visit if you can't get to the office".

As you can see in the example illustrated above, the client has now been cornered into a situation where the answer would quite commonly be," of course, I'd be interested in that; who doesn't want to save money, or at least know if I can save any more? Monday evening sounds perfect".

Not only has the buyer been cornered into answering what the agent wants but he also thinks he is getting something for nothing, a deal!

Bargaining Chips

Should the estate agent fail to secure an appointment through the use of closes, he will wait until he has a "**bargaining chip**". In this case an agent may use your love of a property as a bargaining chip to force you into seeing his financial advisor.

He may say three things to achieve this-

1. That all buyers before making an offer must be financially vetted if they are to purchase through this agency, its company policy.

For example -

" Its our company policy that all buyers see our financial advisor to get financially vetted before purchasing a property; it's a service we provide for the owner, so if you want to buy this house, you have to see my financial advisor. Will you be free on Tuesday or Wednesday?"

2. That the owner of the property has requested the financial advisor sees all buyers. If not, then you will not be able to purchase this property.

For example -

" I know you want the property, but the owner has requested that all buyers be financially vetted by our broker before purchasing. I'm sure you understand; I mean if you were selling a house I'm sure you'd want to make sure the buyer could afford your home and wasn't wasting your time."

3. The estate agent suggests that the buyer see his financial advisor to increase buying power so that they may be able to buy the property they want at the same monthly cost, due to cheaper mortgage deals.

For example -

" Jack, the owner is willing to come down to £ 185,000 but I spoke to my financial advisor and he says that it may be possible to get you that extra £5000 for the same monthly cost, I've already taken the liberty of letting him know; all he wants to know is if he should book you in on Monday or Tuesday evening".

Having employed this bargaining chip successfully to secure the mortgage appointment, more often than not, the financial advisor will succeed in getting the business.

(N.B. conditional selling is illegal under current legislation. All estate agents are aware of this, however many agents tread extremely close to the line or may even cross it to gain maximum profitability from every sale and it is extremely difficult to prove.)

There is no danger in you seeing what the financial advisor has to say. Common sense would direct most people to try to obtain the best possible deal. However, should you choose to make your own mortgage arrangements, you may be severely jeopardising your chances of purchasing your chosen property. An agent's number one objective is profit; they will therefore favour the most profitable client should there be several interested parties on the property. It is common practise for agents to run with so called multiple buyers on a single property to maximise their chances of a successful property sale. A client who utilises the in-house mortgage service will often receive more favourable treatment from the estate agent; those who do not will generally be regarded as "second class" buyers, and leave themselves open to being Gazumped, and as a result, lose money spent on surveyors and legal services.

Tip – Once you have an offer agreed on the property, make an anonymous phone call to the estate agent to see if they are still marketing the property. In the chance that the property is on with a number of agents, call any other agents in the area that may be marketing it to see if they are still accepting viewings on it. This is a good way to see if the property is still being marketed to other buyers and gives you a strong reason to challenge the estate agent in regards to the purchase of the property and the possibility of other buyers.

Tip - Seeing a financial advisor is just like buying a property, have a look at a few before making a decision, and see what else is on offer before choosing one.

Tip - The agent can try and close you any time for a mortgage appointment; estate agent offices can earn as much from mortgages as they do from sales. So an estate agent will continually be hassling you for this appointment. However, he is much more likely to get it once he has gained your trust or has a bargaining chip.

Although there is nothing wrong with seeing another financial advisor, don't forget they are there to sell you something too, so always search for the best deal and never let them force your hand.

Tip - If you have arranged property viewing with an agent, he may ask you for an hour of your time as opposed to describing the properties to you. In particular, if the agent arranges to meet you in his office he may tell you to come 15 minutes earlier so that you can have a quick chat with his financial advisor. This is a common trap that estate agents use to hook in potential clients into financial appointments. They often install the idea into people's heads that it's just a quick chat to see if they can save you any money. Alternatively they may tell you that their financial advisors must financially vet them before being allowed to view any properties, as it is company policy to protect the owners. This is rarely true unless the agent has specific instructions from the owner.

Chapter 6

The Valuation Process and First Impression

On occasion estate agents will receive referrals from people for whom they've sold houses successfully. And in situations like this it's very simple for an agent to get the business with minimal effort. The agent would have already proved himself more than capable in the sale of the referring party and therefore installing the level of confidence required to get the next listing.

However more often than not, the estate agent will have to go through a process during which he will attempt to convince the owner to sell their property through his company and the services they provide. This is called **the Valuation**.

The Valuation Process begins with the **First Impression** as mentioned at the beginning of the book. Just as the estate agent has to make an excellent first impression on a buyer, his impression on a potential vendor must supersede that of the one he is trying to make on a buyer. This is because the Vendor is the one who has the property, pays the agent, and therefore is regarded as the boss!

The estate agent will need to show a huge amount of pro-activity and energy whether on the phone or face to face with a prospective vendor. This is to impress upon the vendor that the agent is pro-active in selling and hungry. And of course who wouldn't want an enthusiastic, energetic, sharp and hungry estate agent to be selling their property? The agent will portray this image from start to finish, as it can make a positive impression on a prospective vendor and indicates the approach the agent may have to the sale of the property. It also serves to inspire a potential vendor to raise his level of interest in what the agent has to say and helps the agent to get one step closer to his goal of the property on the market with his company.

The use of **office assistance** just as with the buyers in the preceding chapters may also come into play here. The property, if listed, will be open to sell by any one of the agents in that office. Therefore at this time it is beneficial to all in the agency, regardless of whether they are working against each other or not. The office assistance may take a number of forms ranging from a cup of tea to a friendly conversation initiated by other members of staff in the office. (Remember the longer the vendor stays in front of the agent, the more time the agent has to build a rapport and sell his services, and hence the greater chance of getting the listing).

Booking and Pre-valuation Questions – Getting Your Private Details

Once the estate agent has identified that you are a vendor, made you feel comfortable and confident in his abilities, and imprinted a good first impression, he will then proceed to ask you a series of pre-valuation questions so that he may discover your current position. The answers you give will aid the agent by giving him adequate information that he can use when on the valuation itself.

What are these questions and why does an agent ask them?

Are you looking to come on the market? – The response to this question will immediately indicate two things to the agent. Firstly whether this is a priority valuation that needs his full attention or whether it's just a standard valuation for someone just wondering about the value of the property or looking to re-mortgage. If it's a standard valuation he will charge you for it.

76

What type of property do you have? – As well as clarifying some property details, this question will be the first in a series of questions that will help the agent come to a basic property valuation based on area, size etc. before he has even seen the property. By knowing the basic make up of the area, property, size, plot etc. the agent will be able to formulate a rough valuation price based on his knowledge of the market before, even stepping into the property.

Where are you looking to move and have you viewed anything yet? - This will tell the agent two things. The first is to see if he can register you as a buyer with either himself or another office he may have. The second is to find out whether you are actively out looking, therefore showing how keen you are about moving house. The quicker you find something you like, the quicker you are likely to sell or take a lower offer on your property.

Why are you selling? – This allows the agent to learn **your current situation.** This could **open up many avenues for the agent to sell and relate to you on,** making you the vendor **more comfortable** with the agent and **more likely to trust him** when it comes the actual valuation as you already share some common ground. For example, if you're selling to retire, the agent will use this to try and relate to your situation. He may tell you his father is retiring and moving to the same area just to build an initial rapport. He may also use the reason for you selling to apply pressure when negotiating a price and accepting an offer.

Any idea on what you think the property is worth yourself? - This question is designed to make the agent's job easy when it comes to valuing your home. By finding out the figure you're looking to achieve half his job is done already. All he has to do is increase it slightly and convince you he can get that price for you.

Are you having any other agents around to value? – This is for the agent to find out his competition and to try and arrange a time where he can be the last to value your home. If the agent is the last one in, then he can not only abuse the other agents, but he knows that if he succeeds where the other agents may have failed, you are more likely to sign with him. A good agent will always try and get in last. Of course this can also backfire and a vendor may sign with another agent first, but usually most people will wait to hear what all the agents they have asked to value the property have to say, before making any decisions.

The agent will also try and find out as much information as possible from you over the phone and build as good a rapport as possible. This not only helps the agent by assessing how serious you are about selling, but the more the prospective vendor is impressed now, the less work needed to build that relationship at the actual valuation. (The extra conversation you have with an agent may also help him to locate your buttons and assess your reactions).

The agent will then grade the valuation on a grade scale of 1,2,3. Grade 1 meaning likely to come on the market, Grade 2 meaning very possible but vendor needs some work and Grade 3 meaning full efforts must be applied to get this one on the market. This gives an indication to the agent valuing what he will need to do and how to approach the valuation as well as giving him all the angles he can use to help his act at the valuation. Once all this is done, all that's left is to book a time.

Overcoming the Fee

"How much do you charge?" This is a very common question that estate agents get and one that many of them prefer not to answer. This is because the estate agent knows that many people are price driven, and so we should be. Why pay more when you can pay less? Estate agents also know this, and because of it often lose business based on what they charge alone, even before a valuation is carried out. Therefore it is the agent's objective to overcome this question in the best way possible, and many of them use one simple tactic, **avoidance**. Agents will do their best to stay clear of any indication of what they charge. A typical example would be: -

Vendor: " what is your commission?"

Agent: " well, we prefer to see the property first as each property is different and we will give you our fee based on the saleability of the property; are you free today or tomorrow for a valuation?"

Here the agent has not only avoided answering the questions but also used the "Or" close in an attempt to get a valuation. In any case most agents have a set fee, so ask them and if they don't give you one, then scare them into telling " if you can't give me your commission rates then, I'll call another agent". This will often be enough for the agent to tell you the fee!

Tip – When calling to book a valuation, always tell the agent that you are looking to put your property on the market, this will almost always guarantee a free valuation. If you tell them that you want a valuation for a re-mortgage or a divorce valuation, then they will always try and charge you for it. And that cash goes straight in the estate agents pocket!

Tip – Many people make a decision on their agent based on the commission they charge. Although the fee is probably the largest factor involved in making your decision, get as many estate agents as possible to come and value your property. This is for two reasons; you will get a more accurate figure on what your property is worth and secondly you can always try and negotiate a lower commission with the agent. But never sign there and then as some agents will try and get you to do. Always take time to think about it and see all the other agents first and keep the fee in mind.

Chapter 7

The Valuation

The Valuation is above all else the most important sale an estate agent will ever have to make. Here he has to convince vendors to trust him with the most valuable asset they may have, their home! The valuation process has only one objective, "to get them to sign where the line is dotted" (*Glenn Gary Glenn Ross*). Although every estate agent has his or her individual approach to a valuation, there are some similarities in the ways in which they deal with prospective vendors and in the closes they may use. In this chapter you will see how these tactics can be executed throughout the process and what to watch out for!

The Agents Act

From the moment you open the front door the agent's act begins. The act is designed to make a vendor feel as confident and comfortable as possible around the estate agent. The estate agent will do his best to woo the vendor through respect, knowledge and courtesy as well as being armed with the information received from the valuation booking stage. He will show a huge amount of energy and pro-activity. This gives the impression that his company consists of a hungry group of estate agents that will perform at their level best to sell your property.

Some agents will often remove their shoes before entering your home as a sign of courtesy and respect. The agent knows that manners give a good impression and go a long way. You may offer the agent a cup of tea or coffee. The agent will always take a cup, this is because the longer he stays, the more likely he is to build a rapport with you and get the property listed.

Next the agent may ask you to give him a tour of the property. He does this for two reasons other than to see the property of course. The first is to see if he can use any of the surroundings to help strengthen the rapport building process. For example, if you're a fireman and he sees a picture of you with your team, then all of a sudden the estate agent will generate a story about how he wanted to be a fireman or that his father is a fireman. Anything he can say that will help him **relate** to the vendor. The greater the relation, the more likely you are to remember him and his company, and the more likely you are to sign with him. (This process is similar to the emotion-spotting tactic we mentioned in chapter 4 and can often relate back to the pre-valuation questions mentioned in the previous chapter.)

The second reason is to use the power of compliments. The agent will very rarely say anything about a property that leads a vendor to believe he will find it a challenge to sell. He will go throughout the property without a single negative comment, telling you how fantastic it is, or all the positives and saleable features it has. Naturally, the more positive attitude an agent has to selling your property, the more he convinces you that he can sell it. Especially if he brings up points that other competing agents may have missed.

The Sale

Once the agent has finished touring the property, he will sit back down with you and begin to sell to you the benefits of using his company. He will tell you about all the tools that they have to increase the chances of sale. These could range from things such as colour advertising, hours they work, web sites they use and all the other things they have that gives them the edge on their competitors.

To accomplish this the estate agent can incorporate two types of closes. The first is the "**benefits**" close. The agent will highlight all the benefits to you as a vendor and how all the things he has to offer will help in the sale of your property. The intention is to highlight all the benefits on offer hoping that one will strike a chord with a vendor.

For example –

" We work longer hours, we have more offices which means we have access to more buyers, we have state of the art computer systems allowing us to find the right buyer for your home and a prime location in the local town. All these things will increase the chances of a quick sale; not having access to all these things in this day and age may minimise your chances".

The intention is to close you on all the benefits so that you feel the agent will be able to sell your property easily and quickly thanks to all the tools available. Also you may notice how the agent uses the "fear of loss" to help him achieve his goal. The agents' intention is subconsciously to plant the idea that by not coming on the market with his company, the vendor will seriously decrease his chances of selling the property and lose out.

The second is the **"Balance sheet"** close. Here the agent may take the opportunity to abuse the other estate agents and to promote his positives. In a way, weighing up the pros and cons in his favour.

For example –

" We work longer hours than any other agency in the area, we have more offices therefore more buyers than any other agency; we are the only agency that offer colour advertising".

The intention behind this is to play all the positives off the negatives of his competitor, thereby convincing the buyer that this agency is the best one to use and pushing the competition out of the picture. (Although you may find that there are a few agents who aren't so subtle and openly abuse their competitors whenever they get the chance).

Nonetheless, the truth is that in this day and age, the ability to sell your own property is becoming more and more widespread. There are a few key factors that a vendor could use to sell their home themselves instead of paying huge commissions to agents for minimal work. With the use of the Internet many people can now advertise their own homes. However if you are feeling a little less confident then there are many internet based estate agents that will market your property on some of the biggest U.K web sites available for a fraction of the price and arrange viewings for you. Current statistics show that nearly 85% of all houses sold are first viewed on the Internet. Other things such as a For Sale board can also be purchased online for as little as £40 in some places, a much smaller amount than having to pay thousands to an agent.

The Price

How does an agent come to the valuation price of your home?

Well many agents already have a pre-meditated price in their heads before you even open the door. This price can sway either way judging on the condition of the property.

However, agents do use **comparables** to help convince you that the value they have given you based on their experience is realistic and accurate. A comparable is a property detail of a house or flat that the estate agent may have sold previously in the area, and bares similarities to that of the one that they are valuing. The agent will use a comparable during the course of the valuation for two reasons. The first is to give some sort of visual evidence to the vendor to support the figure they communicate. The second is as a fall back in the event that they have given a valuation that the vendor is not happy with.

(Estate agents can sometimes change the prices of a comparable to work in their favour, therefore be wary of accepting these documents at face value.)

Over Valuing to Increase the Agents Chances of Getting the Property

Key Opening Tip - Remember that for the majority of us, the purpose of booking a valuation is to find out what our property is worth. However it is widely accepted that 60-70% of all listings go to the agents who value them highest; this purely because money drives many of us, hence if the agent values the property highly, then we make more as vendors. But at the same time an agent may also overvalue a property to justify a high commission. They will often use the argument, " yes we are 1% higher than the other agents, but we can also get you £10,000 more than any other agent." However this can often lead to over valued properties that either sit on the market too long and become stagnant, or end up going through a price reduction process whilst the agent maintains the high commission rate. Therefore it is important that you look into all the factors mentioned in the tips in chapters 6 and 7 rather than just basing your decision on the highest price promised to you.

Giving a valuation that a vendor is unhappy with is a big danger for an estate agent. Therefore an estate agent may at times **overvalue** a property. Over-valuing a property can have two major benefits to the agent.

Firstly by over-valuing the property and convincing the owner it can be sold at that price, the vendor is more likely to go with the agent that can get them more money. Hence the estate agent gets the listing. (Of course, the valuation still has to be reasonable and correspond to the valuation you may have got from the other agents. If one agent

84

values your property at £230,000 and another at £300,000, then obviously there is some malpractice present.) But more often than not, if the agent is the last one in, he can not only sell around other valuations but also successfully communicate a figure that doesn't correspond to current market conditions.

Secondly the estate agent earns more commission if the property sells at a higher price. Unfortunately if the property sells at an over-valued price, then the vendor and agent make money while the buyer is exploited. On the other hand if the property doesn't sell because its too expensive, then the house could end up sitting on the market and becoming stagnant, with prospective buyers not even giving it a second glance. (Obviously this does not benefit the agent either as he loses out on commission or may be dis-instructed. However, in order to overcome this he may use tactical price reductions to lower the price of the property, once he has it on his books. This will be discussed in the following chapter).

The Fee/The Commission

The most important question that needs to be answered by an estate agent is *How much is your commission?* Many of us feel that the fee we pay to an agent is much greater than the job done by them. But as the primary objective of any business is to maximise profits. The agent has to overcome any objections to the fee in order to get as high a commission as possible. He can usually accomplish this with one of three different approaches.

The first is to convince you that based on all the **Benefits** the company has to offer the fee is justified and needs to be high in order to cover the costs of such benefits. And if the agency has enough to offer then this will make logical sense to the vendor to go with the suggested fee.

The second called **The Price Covers The Fee** is the most commonly used approach. An estate agent will often tell the vendor that they can increase the price of the property, therefore in the event of a sale, the fee will automatically be covered by the sale price. This gives the vendor the impression that the commission the agent charges will be covered within the sale and at no loss to them, and hence is justifiable. Of course this is not always the case, and nobody knows how circumstances can change and what the vendor will be willing to accept a few weeks down the line. More often than not the vendor will have to come down in price based on viewer feedback whilst the commission remains the same.

The third is the **Match the Fee approach**. Here the estate agent will offer to match the fee of one of the other agents that have already valued the property, while at the same time highlighting all the extra benefits on offer. This makes vendors believe they are getting more value for their money and could be enough to convince an owner to come on the market with that agent.

Once the agent has gone through this process, he will summarise all the points and then ask you for the business. An estate agent will always ask you for the business. Many agents believe this is the most effective close in this situation; if you don't ask, you don't get!

Tip - Always remember that the agent is the one that needs your property to make his money. You are the one in control, its up to him to get your business. This in turn increases your power of negotiation. Because he needs you more, and does not want you to go on the market with his competitors, he is more likely to negotiate on a lower fee. You must remember that all estate agents are negotiators and the chances are that he already has a set figure in his mind of what he is willing to go down too. So your objective is to get that fee down

as low as possible. It's your property you have the control. They need you more than you need them!

Tip - Never sign there and then, always see a few agents and take your time to make a decision, don't feel pressured to make a decision there and then, make them wait a day.

Tip - A common tactic used by agents before signing is to state that they have a minimum contract term of X weeks. In reality, this is not the case; it's merely another sales tactic, firstly to give the agent maximum exclusivity for selling time and the second is to freeze out the competition from getting to sell the property. The contract can be amended, so be aware! Many agents will have exhausted their client bank within the first week of marketing. Therefore it is advisable to negotiate as short a term as possible and to allow a greater degree of flexibility should your first chosen agent fail to deliver a buyer. Don't be afraid to ask for a shorter contract term.

Other Closes an Agent Could Use

Although this process seems quite straightforward the agent can always use a number of closes throughout the valuation process to accompany and support his approach and in turn slowly nudge you into a making a decision in his favour.

" We had a buyer" close – The "We had a buyer" close is used with a sense of urgency and a fear of loss to make it effective. The estate agent will often say things like, " we just had a buyer that was looking for a property in this road". The aim is to make the owner believe that the agent has access to the type of people who can buy his property. The agent may at times incorporate a degree of office assistance here to strengthen this idea. He may call his office in front of the potential vendor and ask the agents if any of them have a buyer that is looking for such a home.

He will tell the owner that they have a buyer or a number of buyers who are looking for that type of property, in that sort of price-range. But the catch is that in order to arrange such beneficial viewing on the property, the vendor would have to sign with the agency.

Naturally this can put the vendor under pressure; if he wants to sell his home he may be pushed to sign the contract as soon as possible, otherwise he may lose out on prospective buyers. Once the so-called beneficial viewing is arranged, it is very possible the buyer may not like the property (especially if it is a mock viewing). However the agent now has a signed contract that ties the owner in for a number of weeks, which is enough time for the agent to try and sell the property, whilst maintaining exclusivity for the property.

" The Mock Viewing and Offer" Tactic – This occurs when an agent tells the vendor they have an interested buyer and ask for a one off viewing without any contracts. If the viewing is successful the owner can proceed with the sale, if not then they can choose another agent. The agent then as in the example above may use office assistance to create an awareness of a potential buyer. Then the agent can arrange a mock viewing unknown to the vendor on the condition that if it is successful, then the vendor can sign with his company. Once the viewing takes place the prospective buyer offers. The vendor is forced to sign with the agent. Then of course the buyer pulls out and the agent is left with a signed contract.

"Best Time to Sell" Close - This is when the estate agent aims to convince the owner that it is the best time to sell the property. Using outside factors, such as a danger of increase in interest rates, a sudden rise in the level of U.K buyers or the current increase in sales in the surrounding area. The agent will try and nudge a potential vendor who may only be considering selling into a situation where they feel it is imperative for them to sell and by not coming on the market they may lose out on all the benefits the current market conditions have exposed.

For example - " buyers are at an all time high at the moment, as are prices and many of them are particularly interested in your area because of schooling. If you want to maximise your chances of selling, it's the best time to sell".

" Negative Consequences" Close – This close works in reverse to the best time to sell close. As opposed to highlighting the benefits of selling, it highlights the danger of not selling now.

For example -

" Buyers are at an all time high at the moment, as are prices and many of them are particularly interested in your area because of schooling. However there are talks of an increase in interest rates, so this high level of interest could drop at any time so if you don't want to lose out, its best to come on the market as soon as possible".

Demonstration Close - The demonstration close is an accompanying close more than anything else. An estate agent will often try and impress you on the way in which he sells your property by giving you a demonstration of a viewing on your own property during the valuation. If he does it well enough to convince you to buy property, then he may have gained the confidence required for you to instruct him.

Companion Close – The companion close as mentioned previously is in this case focused on selling the benefits of using the agency to the other person(s) in the room that show greater interest in the services provided by the agency. The agent will focus his sales efforts on just one person in the hope that they will then sell it to their spouse or partner later on under a less pressured environment.

For example –

Mrs X. – " But Honey, I really thought that the last agent was the best of all, I know you're not too keen on their commission but I really think they have the best approach and a lot more tools in comparison with the other agents. And I'm sure they'll be able to sell it, plus his dad was a fireman just like yours!"

Condition Close – The condition close can be identified by four words, " if you, then I". An agent will often offer certain conditions to the vendor to help them close on the valuation. It is often quite effective with the promise of a gift or service. The aim is to limit the vendors' resistance to any ideas the agent may put forward by making him an offer and giving him the choice.

For example - " if you come on the market with us, then I will match the other agents fee and Ill throw in a weekend trip for you and your wife at a health spa".

Quality of Agent Close – The quality of agent close is another accompanying close. It is used as a support by the agent to convince a vendor that by going with them they will be benefiting from an agent that has been established in the area for a very long time, and that the quality of their service is second to none. In this case you need to ask yourself one question, how many buyers care as to how long an agent has been established? The only thing you as a vendor want to know is can the agent sell it and how quickly?

Special Deal for a Special Customer Close – This close can often be used by an estate agent when trying to close the prospective vendor for a fee. The agent will often try and close the vendor with the idea that they are offering them a special deal that is exclusive to just that one person or a specific time period. This makes the vendor feel that again they are getting more value for money as well as feeling quite important and exclusive.

For example -

" Mr.X I am willing to give you a special 1% commission rate if you sign with me today and today only. I am aware that other agents have offered you the same but I'm sure you'll agree none of them offer what we offer and you'll be getting so much more in terms of service and quality. I've never made an offer to anyone like this before; you're the first. Our standard sole agency fee is usually 2% but because I like you so much I'm willing to budge on this, but I have to know by today by 7pm because after that it will go back to 2%".

Yes Yes Close – The "Yes Yes" close is a psychological close that an agent may use to help his chances of getting your business. The agent will ask you a series of questions, to which every answer of yours will be "yes". Once the agent has put you in a repetitive pattern of saying yes over and over again, the chances of your saying yes to the next question increase dramatically. As crazy as it sounds, it does work on occasion. Hence when the agent finally asks you for the business, you may just say "Yes!"

Repetition Close – The repetition close is a way in which an agent uses repetition to keep you thinking about himself and his company. For example, if someone says to you " a rat can go longer without water than a camel " twelve times, you are more likely to remember this fact. An estate agent can close you in a similar way into remembering his company by mentioning the company name over and over. This will keep the name of the company highlighted in your head and play a role when you are trying to decide later on which agent to sign with. People will often put more memorable things in a list of options than those they cannot recall.

Adjournment Close – The adjournment close is used to give the vendor time to consider all the options without feeling as though they were in a pressured environment. Very much like a Jury in a courthouse. However by using other closes such as the benefits close and the repetition close in conjunction with this one, it can work as a helpful tool when the vendor reflects on all the agents they have seen.

For example – " at X estate agents we accompany all viewing", if this is a benefit that appeals to the owner and is repeated enough times, then the owner may lean towards that agent when considering his choices and making a decision in his own time.

Bully Close – Unfortunately this is one of the most disgusting closes any sales person can use. The agent will at times railroad a vendor into signing a contract. This will often happen in the case where the vendor is an elderly or incapable person. The agent will take full advantage of their situation and literally bully them into signing an agreement for a high commission and huge length of time on the contract.

Tip – If you are elderly or incapable then make sure you have someone you trust a family member or friend present when dealing with the estate agent. Similarly if you know of someone who is elderly and is considering selling his or her property then make sure you are present so that there is less chance for the estate agent to use the bully close.

The main objective is for the agent to get the property on the market and a signed contract. This is because the most important thing for an agent to keep his head above water is the amount of properties he has on his books. "If you throw enough mud at a wall, some of it will stick". Agents work in a similar way; if they have enough properties, then they will sell enough properties, it's as simple as that.

Tip - Although the agent may use all these closes to try and get you to sign, the one underlying tip for all these closes is take your time and do your research. Regardless of what the agent says, take time to make an informed decision and use that time to research the agent thoroughly; check their advertising, sold boards, newspapers, property particulars, descriptive texts and links with other big national web sites. Don't sign there and then, you always have the advantage as the vendor. Remember the most important things to you should not be what he's said or how he's said it. It should be did he give a correct valuation, can he sell it, how quickly and are the commission and terms of the contract reasonable?

Tip – A good tactic which a vendor can use to get a lower fee is the play-off close. This is where the vendor plays one agent off against another. A vendor could say something like, " We have seen a few agents and we've narrowed our choice down to you and one other agent. We would prefer to go on the market with you but the other agent has offered us a lower fee of X% commission, if you can match that deal then we will come on the market with you. If you cant then I'm afraid we will have to go on the market with the other agent". Always remember to smile when closing your agent with the play-off close.

Tip - When choosing your agent take the time period that I mentioned previously and use it constructively. Don't just wait a day and sign it 24 hours later. Do a background check on the points the agent has tried to sell you on. Take a drive around the area and have a look at how many boards have the word "SOLD", on them. Look at their advertising particulars, their web site, and their ads in the paper and ask yourself, " would it inspire me if I was a buyer?" Look at the words and ways in which they describe properties. When viewing pictures of other properties they may have on their books, look out for things such as brown leaves or snow, if its summer, then you'll know how long some of their properties have been on the market. Check to see if the agents are interlinked on large property web sites that give access to buyers from all over the country so as to increase the chances of a sale.

Chapter 8

Price Reductions and the Illusion of Vendor Care

In the last chapter we spoke about how some agents overvalued properties in order to get them on to the market. Selling an overvalued property is a great success for the estate agent, as he will earn a higher commission. But, if a property is too expensive, then nobody will buy it, and the agent would lose out altogether. The way in which an agent can overcome this is through **Price Reductions**. Agents will often try and get the market price of a property reduced so that the chances of a sale become greatly increased, especially if they overvalued it in the first place. The price reduction is not an instant process. The decision to reduce a price is made by a vendor not the agent. Therefore the agent has to put forward enough reasons over a period of time to convince the vendor that a price reduction is the best way to go. Agents can sometimes use unorthodox tactics to speed this process up as well as to support any reasons they may give to a vendor in regards to the idea of a price reduction. What follows are a number of ways in which the agent will try and accomplish the price reduction.

Mock Viewing and Negative Feedback

As we mentioned in the earlier chapters, estate agents will often pay more attention to buyers that are in a good position to proceed with a sale. However, some agents keep a few " time-wasters" on their books for **mock viewing** on properties.

A number of mock viewings can be a useful tool for an agent. An estate agent will often book viewing for properties with the " time wasters" but tell the vendor that they are all buyers that are in an excellent position to purchase. More often than not these viewings result in nothing but time wasting for the owner. However they also serve another purpose. The estate agent can use these mock viewings to his advantage to create negative feedback that he communicates back to the vendor. The negative feedback can be useful in planting the idea of a price reduction with the vendor. On each of the feedback comments the estate agent may also give a number of reasons as to why the people viewing didn't like the property, to accompany the angle he is trying to take. The estate agent will have a number of different ways in which he can communicate the negative feedback but will almost always accompany these comments with a degree of disappointment, shock or awe.

For example -

" Hey Terry, its John from the estate agents. I've spoken to the couple who viewed last night and I've got some feedback for you. Now…they liked the property, however . . . they said to me that they felt it was a little expensive. Now I was very surprised they said that and don't agree in the slightest. To tell you the truth I was a bit embarrassed to have to tell you what they said. However it is our company policy to provide you with feedback! But I wouldn't worry too much, its still early days, we have a another viewing coming up, let's hope we have a better result this time."

If the house remains on the market for a long period of time, the vendor may become very anxious and open to ideas about how to stimulate a greater interest for his property. If there is enough negative feedback communicated to the vendor accompanied by good reasons after each viewing, then the chances of a price reduction increase heavily. If the price reduction fails on the first attempt, the negative feedback may serve well to pre-sell the idea of a price reduction, therefore making it even simpler for the agent to achieve this without any major objections or resistance later on.

Vendor Care Calls

Estate agents will often have allocated phone times where they contact the owners. This is to maintain communication with the owner and to keep them updated as to how the marketing of the property is going. This is known as **vendor care calling**. However there can be a hidden agenda with vendor care.

The estate agent may use vendor care calls to try and reduce the price of a property. Unlike feedback comments that are given separately after each viewing, the vendor care call will focus on a much stronger approach whereby all feedback and comments are communicated in one hit. The agent achieves this by giving a summary of all the viewing feedback as well as putting forward any other information he can use that will help move towards a price reduction. (The agent may also use things such as Internet viewing statistics about the property and other such data to help him achieve this).

The agent will often communicate this information stating the different reasons for the lack of interest, making particular reference to the price. Also, he will highlight to the vendor how it is his aim to work with the owner to find ways to generate a greater level of interest in the property. He will promote the idea that the sale of the property is just as beneficial to him as it is to the owner because he wants to make money too. Although this is true the agent doesn't want to arouse suspicion with the owner as to his intentions. Therefore he will make it seem as though it is his aim to work with the owner to achieve a greater interest and a successful sale as opposed to just getting a price reduction.

For example -

" Hi Terry, I'm just calling to discuss how things are going with the property. Obviously we haven't sold it yet and I'm calling to try and see how we can work together to generate a greater level of interest. So far we've had 7 viewings on the property and for the most part the feedback seems to be quite similar for all that have viewed. They all like the property, the décor and the location; however the common barrier seems to be the price. I also have in front of me the Internet statistics that show how many people have clicked on your property online and from that how many have requested details or viewing. And the click rate is not as high as we'd originally hoped. The sale of your property is just as beneficial to me as it is to you; otherwise I won't earn any money myself. So I'm just wondering how we can work together to resolve this, and if you had any ideas or suggestions that we could implement What are your thoughts?"

The example above shows how the agent implemented what we mentioned above and used a type of subtle" **price reduction**" close by which he lists all the feedback that has been received about the property and stating the one common negative barrier with all comments. He then supports this point with Internet statistics. The aim is to limit the owner's options so that he is nudged towards the only logical choice based on the feedback given from buyers, which in this case would be a price reduction.

Tip - A good tip to throw the agent off guard is the idea of parallel reduction. If you have to reduce the price on your property, then the agent should be willing to reduce his commission. Remember that you have employed the agent to sell your property for as close to the valued figure as possible. If you have to take a hit in the pocket, then why shouldn't he! If you lower your sale price, then he should lower his commission. If he doesn't then instruct another agent as soon as your

contract term is up. Which as mentioned in the previous chapter should be kept as short as possible depending on the market. And make sure that if you do negotiate a new price then you make the relevant changes to both copies of the agreement you have with the estate agency. Failing that you can make a new agreement but be sure that all the copies of the previous one are destroyed. Also make sure the remaining time period stays the same on the new contract, if the agent only has two weeks left to sell your property then make sure he puts down just two weeks. Remember you're the vendor, he needs your business so you have the upper hand in this negotiation. You have the power so don't be afraid to use it!

Fake Offers for a Price Reduction

Another tactic that is often used is the **fake offer** tactic. The estate agent could arrange a viewing and communicate a fake offer to the vendor. This offer will indicate to the owner what a buyer thinks the property is worth. The agent could use this in the vendor care call and if there are enough such offers or negative feedback to support a lower price then the vendor is more likely to lean towards a price reduction.

If the vendor decides to accept the fake offer, then the estate agent can very easily make that buyer disappear with a bad news phone call by, saying such things as " they found a different property" or " the buyer has pulled out due to personal problems". Therefore the fake offer tactic can serve a very useful purpose when trying to obtain a price reduction.

Tip – There is no substitute for your own legwork. Always try and find out what the market growth is in your area and do your sums to have an idea of what your property is worth. Don't just take the agents word for it; of course a good estate agent can give you a more

accurate valuation, but have a rough figure in your head. There are also number of Internet web sites that give information statistics for property growth as well as schools and crime rates.

Chapter 9

Other Sales Tools an Estate Agent May Use

As well as using closes, estate agents can use a number of sales skills that are naked to the eye. These skills help in giving the estate agent a greater edge over the client without the client ever being aware. Studies have shown that words have a 7% influence on our behaviour and thoughts, voice quality and tone have a 38% influence and that physiology has a 55% influence. So for the majority of sales, people tend to focus and respond more to the way in which an estate agent says something and uses his physiology as opposed to what is actually being said. So how does the agent do this?

Words- 7%

Word Arrangements

Some estate agents attempt to plant a seed in the mind of a buyer to help them with their sales approach. In order to do this they often use Word Arrangements. As I mentioned in chapter two, almost everything an agent says is pre-programmed or planned with an objective in place. An agent may use word arrangements in a similar way with the use of repetition in a sentence to highlight something he wants the buyer to know or think.

For example -

"How long have you been looking to buy? South Beach is becoming a very popular area to buy in; many people are buying there at the moment. What kind of property are you looking to buy and have you considered buying in South Beach?"

As you can see in the example above the estate agent has asked a few questions that may be quite common at the beginning of the sales process. However hidden within these questions are a few key words that have been arranged in a specific way so that they will be subconsciously implanted in a buyer's thoughts with the use of repetition. The estate agent continually uses the words **Buy and South Beach.**

By repeating these words throughout questions and statements, the estate agent hopes subconsciously to implant the words **BUY, SOUTH BEACH, BUY, SOUTH BEACH!** An agent may use this kind of tactic in a number of different variations so keep an eye out for repetitive highlighted words.

Word Associations

Word Association is a tool that an agent uses to influence the behaviour of a buyer through the use of language and the way in which it is communicated. This plays a greater role than people are aware. Very simply put, word association works by using words to stimulate emotions and communicate images in the mind of a buyer.

The estate agent will use specific words and phrases in which to communicate different points so that the behavioural reaction a client has to them will lean in the estate agent's favour.

For example -

Describing a room in a house as cosy is a lot different from calling it small.

Or

Going into a café and ordering a bottle of mineral water is a lot different from asking for a drink of water.

As you can see the different words or ways used to describe or communicate the same thing can play differently in the way in which it is perceived.

The aim is to cushion or influence a particular emotion or thought a potential buyer may have to a negative aspect of the property, so that it may be less harmful to the sale. So watch out for the word transformations.

Socio-linguistics- Voice Quality and Tone –38%

Many of us can relate to Socio-linguistics. We often use it in everyday situations where we vary the way in which we communicate verbally to those around us. For example, the way in which we speak to an employer will be vastly different from the baby talk we use to speak to an infant.

Similarly the way in which an estate agent puts his point across is one of the most important aspects of his sales approach. The way in which he speaks can vary from client to client. Surprisingly studies have shown that 38% of people react to the voice quality and tone a sales person uses to communicate a point. This point may sound simple; however it plays a major part in a client's mind as to how professional, educated and trustworthy a sales person they are dealing with.

For example: - how many of you would seriously consider a sales pitch from an agent that spoke like an infant and how many of you would consider one communicated from an agent with a knowledgeable, sophisticated and professional tone?

As you can see from the example illustrated above, many of us would find it a challenge to have faith in an estate agent that could not communicate his point in a clear and professional manner.

Physiology- 55%

Physiology plays the greatest role in sales; up to 55%. An estate agent will often use his physiology in the form of mirrors to give the impression that he and the client are just two normal people discussing property as opposed to sales professional and client. As mentioned in chapter 2, it is important for the estate agent to dissolve any resistance and build a relationship of trust with the client, particularly on common interests when possible. This is because the better the trust the more chance of a sale. The estate agent will often mimic elements of a client's body language, ranging from hand gestures to breathing and posture to help create a more comfortable atmosphere and relate to the client.

For example -

If you belch at a dinner table it can be considered rude by the other people there. But if they all begin belching straight after you, you automatically feel comfortable in your surroundings.

In a similar way estate agents will often mirror your movements and body language to keep you comfortable and relaxed as well as feeling as though you are on the same level as each other. If the client use a thumbs-up gesture, an estate agent may do the same, if you rest your chin on your hand when leaning forward to look at property details on his desk, he will do the same. If you are a smoker, he might light a cigarette to keep you company.

Humour

Humour plays one of the most important roles when it comes to relaxing a buyer and reducing resistance. As you can imagine for an agent this can be vital. Many estate agents use humour to make clients feel comfortable and to put them into a good state of mind. Keeping a client laughing not only reduces their resistance to the estate agent but also makes them open to further options. It also makes the client associate positive feelings with that estate agent. This increases the chances of a sale for the agent, whether it is selling a property or selling their services at a valuation. (Humour will also make the estate agent a lot more memorable serving a positive purpose in regards to future recommendations or referrals).

Chapter 10

Estate Agents and Their Relationships

Throughout the book we mentioned how estate agents benefit from sales and mortgages. In addition to this estate agents can also benefit from individual parties that function independently of the estate agency itself. However, these parties can often inter-link with the process of a sale.

The outside parties can be investors, recommended conveyancers, timber and damp specialists, roof specialists, plumbers and electricians.

Relationships with Investors

Many estate agents deal with investors on a regular basis. An investor could be a number of different persons. An investor may take the form of the estate agency itself or the estate agent (here both would have to declare their interest). It could also be a friend or relative of the agent that is purchasing on behalf of the estate agent incognito or it may be an independent investor. Although there are many investors who will buy properties honestly and based on the correct market value, there are a few that estate agents work with so that they can benefit from the sale of the property two fold.

The benefit gained other than the commission from the sale is that the estate agent may receive back handers also known as "drinks" in return for getting the investor a reduced price on the property. These "drinks" can often be sums in the thousands and are much more appealing to an estate agent than just a standard commission alone that may only be hundreds of pounds. This practise is illegal but very common among some estate agents and their investors. These estate agents put the interests of the investor before the interests of their vendors and do what they can to get the investor the best deal, while the vendor loses out.

So to What Lengths will an Estate Agent go to get the Best Price? He Under-values!

The estate agent may **Under-value** a property. If an estate agent is successful in building an excellent rapport and trust at the valuation as well as closing you on the benefits of using his company, he will use that trust and faith that you have in him to undervalue your property. By undervaluing a property and offering it to an investor the estate agent will receive his "drink" and the investor will make a profit from the re-sale of the property.

But doesn't the agent lose out on commission? No, he doesn't as explained in the following example:

If an estate agency charged 2% on a £250,000 property the commission would be £5000. The individual estate agent may get a 10% commission of that fee, which would entitle him to £500.

Now imagine there is a £5000 drink for a £50,000 under-valuation from the investor.

2% at £200,000 = £4000 for the estate agency, and the estate agent earning a 10% commission of that fee would be £400. With the commission + £5000 drink = £5400.

The estate agent could earn up to £5400 in total for dropping the price by £50,000. And the investor has made a £45,000 profit.

As you can see from the example above, the vendor can often lose out and the estate agent gains greatly at his expense.

(At times the estate agent receiving the drink may split it so to cover any commission lost by the estate agency due to a reduction in the price. In the example above it was £ 1000 loss for the agency itself, but if the drink was split 40/60 between the agent and his company then the agency would receive an extra £1000 over the fee they would have got having sold it at the true market value price).

NB. Remember the surveyor works solely on behalf of the purchaser and their chosen lender. Therefore, if the property is being sold at below market average, i.e. it has been undervalued, it is relatively unlikely that this would be raised as a point with the property vendor.

Tip - If you are concerned that the estate agent is undervaluing or has undervalued your property, the best thing to do is to get several agents in to value the property. On top of this you can also find out the market growth in your area and calculate a rough value of what you think your property is worth and see if the agents come up with a similar figure. As a last resort, if you are suspicious of malpractice by the estate agent in the valuation you can get a friend or relative to put in an offer anonymously and see how the estate agent communicates it to you, or whether he communicates it at all. This could be a good indication of whether he is trying to under-value the property so he can offer it to an investor.

Relationships with Recommended Conveyancers

Estate agency and conveyancing come hand in hand during the sale of a property. For this reason some estate agents work with specific conveyancing companies. This is for two reasons; not only will the estate agency be able to earn a commission from the placement, as well as a commission for the individual agent, but the estate agency can often regulate this sale more closely.

Many of these companies provide a more than adequate service for the conveyancing of the sale. Unfortunately there are also many that even though they are much cheaper than paying a normal solicitor tend to provide a less than adequate service which can in turn create an unnecessary amount of anxiety for the people involved and has at times caused sales to fall through. They may often delay communication between parties relevant to the sale and cause uncertainty between buyers and sellers as well as causing unnecessary pressure on the sale and others in the chain.

Tip - Try and find out as much information as possible about the recommended conveyancing companies offered to you by the estate agent, before making any decisions. Some of these companies are very good but make sure you do a thorough background check before appointing them to act for you. However the best option is to appoint a reputable local solicitor who has a good knowledge of the area; it may be more expensive, but it's a small price to pay for the reduced level of anxiety, peace of mind and the chances of a more secure transaction.

Relationships with Timber and Damp Specialists, Roof Specialists, Plumbers and Electricians

On occasion an estate agent may be faced with a situation where a property he has sold has performed poorly in a specific area on a survey. Re-negotiating a price that would cover the cost of repairing this problem can often solve many of these issues. However there are times where an estate agent can face losing the sale altogether.

In a situation like this there is a certain amount of action an estate agent can take to secure his sale. These issues could involve things such as timber and damp problems or roof problems etc. In order to overcome this problem the estate agent may have relationships with some of the professionals that he uses. The estate agent could recommend or even arrange these specialists on behalf of the buyer to assess the problem. The estate agent will then offer a " drink" to this specialist so that he may put forward a favourable report to the buyer, thereby reducing the level of anxiety and increasing the chances of securing the sale again.

Tip - The best option is to appoint a specialist independent to that of the recommendations of the estate agent. This will ensure that you receive an objective and untainted report about the problem that has been raised on your survey and will enable you to make a decision without unknown influential factors.

Chapter 11

Introduction to the Home Information Pack (H.I.P)

What is the (H.I.P)?

As of 1st of June 2007 new government legislation will be brought into full effect whereby home sellers will have to provide an information pack known as the Home Information Pack (H.I.P) for buyers. The aim of this pack is to improve the process of purchasing a home in England and Wales. This will be achieved by bringing together all the information people need to know in order to buy a home so that they may make an informed decision on what may be the biggest investment of their lives.

Home-owners or their chosen estate agent will be required to have an H.I.P before marketing a property for sale and to make this pack available to prospective buyers.

The information the pack is likely to include is as follows: -

- Evidence of Title
- The Terms of Sale
- Standard searches
- A Home Condition Report based on a survey of the property
- Energy Performance Certificate (which will report upon the properties energy efficiency)
- Where the property is a Leasehold - a copy of the lease as well as information on service charges and insurance
- A New Homes Warranty and Guarantees for new properties

- Where the property is Commonhold – commonhold information, copy of commonhold community statement

The Pros of the H.I.P

- The H.I.P will provide relevant information on properties allowing prospective purchasers to make more informed decisions.
- The H.I.P will filter out anyone not serious about selling and therefore the market will consist of people who are serious about selling as opposed to those just curious about the market response their property would receive were they to only consider selling.
- First time buyers will receive the packs free of charge therefore reducing the cost of getting on the property ladder.
- The pack is aimed at reducing the anxiety involved in buying and selling.
- Estate agents that provide the H.I.P will be required to be part of a regulated redress scheme therefore improving the quality of service and increasing consumer confidence.

The Cons of the H.I.P

- It may take up to two weeks for a seller to arrange the documentation for the H.I.P. Some argue this would reduce the number of properties coming on the market and therefore gazumping may increase, as buyers will be more likely to fight over the same property.
- Buyers lack of confidence in the survey provided by the sellers might force them to have an independent survey done anyway, therefore incurring more cost.
- Sellers may choose to increase the marketing or sale price of their properties to cover the costs of the H.I.P.
- Sellers will have to pay for the H.I.P, prices could range between £600-£1000.

- In a slow market, things such as searches may go out of date forcing the seller to reapply and spend more money.
- If the property does not sell, then the vendor will be out of pocket as a result of money spent on the H.I.P.
- Some argue, that a possible reduction of properties on the market due to time scale of preparing the H.I.P. and the cost involved could cause inflation in property prices.
- Estate agents could increase their commission to cover the cost of co-ordinating an H.I.P. for a seller.
- People selling their property without an H.I.P may be subject to a fine.

Tip - Many agents may use a " no stress" close in order to increase the chances of getting the property. They will reassure the vendor that they will take care of any concerns regarding the new developments in the property market. They may also make the H.I.P. out to be more complicated than it actually is and increase commissions as a result of having to co-ordinate such a "complicated" new development.

Tip - If you do choose an estate agent that provides the H.I.P make sure that they are part of the certified redress scheme.

Sources

1. BBC Programme, The Secret Agent, 21st March 2006
2. ITV Programme, Confessions of an Estate Agent, 20th February 2007
3. Website: www.Homeinformationpack.go.uk
4. BBC News Web Site. 13th April 2006